SWEET WINES

SWEET WINES

A GUIDE TO THE WORLD'S BEST
WITH RECIPES

JAMES PETERSON

STEWART, TABORI & CHANG
NEW YORK

Published in 2002 by
Stewart, Tabori & Chang
A Company of La Martinière Groupe
115 West 18th Street
New York, NY 10011

Export Sales to all countries except Canada, France,
and French-speaking Switzerland:
Thames and Hudson Ltd.
181A High Holborn
London WC1V 7QX
England

Library of Congress Cataloging-in-Publication Data

Peterson, James.
    Sweet wines : a guide to the world's best with recipes / James
Peterson.
        p. cm.
    Includes indexes.
    ISBN 1-58479-255-8
        1. Wine and wine making. 2. Cookery (Wine) I. Title.

TP548.P44 2002
641.2'2—dc21   2002075753

Printed in China

10 9 8 7 6 5 4 3 2 1

First Printing

Designed by Hotfoot Studio

ACKNOWLEDGMENTS

My deep thanks to the myriad people, from South Africa to Canada to Australia, who have been forthcoming with information, insight, and wines. Although you are too numerous to list, your contributions were essential in bringing this book to fruition.

I'd like to thank Joshua Eisen, wine expert, who read the manuscript and spotted omissions and ambiguities. Josh also helped me track down some rare and unusual wines. Becky Sue Epstein has a passion for sweet wines and a deep knowledge of them; she helped me make some important contacts. Neal Rosenthal of Rosenthal Wine Merchant, a friend and connoisseur, supplied me with information and some rare and delicious wines. Victor Schwartz of VOS Selections introduced me to the great wines of Hungary. John Schreiner was pivotal in tracking down Canadian wines, which can be hard to find in the United States—a condition that hopefully will change. Thank you Mannie Berk of The Rare Wine Company for letting me have a bottle of 1834 Madeira at a price I could afford.

Most readers would be amazed by the amount of work and talent it takes to bring a manuscript from rough, typewritten pages to the finished book. I'd like to thank my editor and publisher, Leslie Stoker, for always being encouraging and upbeat even when she had criticism to deliver. Sarah Scheffel worked very closely on the manuscript and layouts, making sure everything was in the right place and going over it innumerable times. This book could not exist without her. Thank you Tanya Ross-Hughes of Hotfoot Studio for your artful eye and your beautiful design. Ann O'Connor, the excellent copy editor, so profoundly attentive to detail, deserves high praise for spotting errors and oversights. The infinitely skillful Kim Tyner, production manager, is responsible for the beautiful print quality, so rare in books about wine. And thank you Jack Lamplough for helping to promote not only this book, but my others as well.

Many thanks to Stephanie Shapiro for testing all the recipes—you were beyond conscientous. Then there are those who helped me with the pictures. Ann Disrude, food stylist par excellence, thank you for your talent, good humor, and those wonderful lunches. And thank you Tracy Harlor for helping out in the kitchen. Debre DeMers, photo assistant, thank you for your laughter and your encouragement. Most of all, thank you for being my friend.

Thank you Elise and Arnold Goodman, my agents, for helping me keep my head above water (or above wine) when the long days of working alone sometimes got me down. I am moved by your commitment to me and to what I do. Finally thank you to my partner, Zelik, for being there and for being who you are.

Preface

As a boy I went to a Catholic school and to mass every Sunday. In those days the mass was in Latin, and while most of it was incomprehensible to me, it always exerted a certain fascination. The ritual of the mass and its surrounding iconography continue to intrigue me, and I suspect they are related to my fascination with food, more specifically bread and wine, the central transformation symbols of Christianity, Judaism, and, long ago, of paganism. There remains something sacred about sipping wine and breaking bread, especially with others. Wine lifts the spirits and nurtures the soul.

Hence, it is with a certain reverence that I approach wine and the act of sharing wine and food with friends. Wine demands our attention. Wine is not like a soft drink of which every sip and every bottle is the same, but rather is different at each moment, from bottle to bottle and sip to sip. Winemaking is an art so closely allied with nature that it can affect us in the same way that a painting or piece of music can, while at the same time awakening our appreciation of natural beauty. Throughout most of Western civilization, the senses and the soul have inhabited different domains that more often than not have been at odds with one another. The notions of sacrifice and deprivation have become associated with goodness, and the pursuit of pleasure somehow with the work of the Devil. But this wasn't always so. The ancient Greeks had Dionysus, the god of wine, dance, and passion, who expressed both the light and dark sides of human nature. He gave license to excess and made the sensual sacred. I wish we could have him back.

It's very likely that in the time of the ancient Greeks and Romans, many wines, especially the best wines, were sweet. Because dry wines are quickly susceptible to air, to changes in temperature, and to movement, they wouldn't have kept well in an era that predated glass bottles and corks. Corks didn't become standard until the 16th century, and it was only then that dry wines could be kept for long periods of time, transported with relative ease, and benefit from being aged in the bottle. Many sweet wines, on the other hand, benefit from exposure to air, which gives them an oxidized quality that's an essential part of their identity. Many sweet wines are, to this day, aged in barrels with air remaining in them and at times are even left out in the sun. Because sugar and acid, which are both present in large amounts in sweet wines, act as preservatives, some sweet wines can be kept for relatively long periods of time without undergoing any perceptible change. This is in fact one of the great advantages to serving sweet wines—you can serve a little and keep the rest in the refrigerator for days or even weeks. (Only some sweet wines, specifically vintage-dated red wines, should be drunk, like dry wines, at a single sitting.) All wines benefit from a squirt of oxygenless air once opened (see Keeping Your Wine Fresh After You've Opened It, page 113).

We live in an era when wine is fashionable and many of the old standbys, such as a good bottle of Bordeaux or Burgundy, have become so expensive that they're hard to enjoy. My own way of dealing with this ever-worsening situation is to keep ahead of the pack by looking for wines that are so little known that I can afford them. Each year it is harder to find a bottle of truly great wine without feeling the sting of the price. While sweet wines are rarely cheap—in fact some have become frightfully expensive—they still offer us access to wines of great depth and complexity for maybe a tenth of the price of a comparably complex dry wine.

But I know from the perplexed looks I get when I say I'm writing a book about sweet wines that many of us shrink away when we hear that a wine is sweet. It has in fact become fashionable to prefer dry wines, as though sweet wines were for amateurs. This may be because for years cheap wines were sold more or less sweet, no doubt in part to cover up poor quality. Until 1968, more sweet wine was made in California than dry wine, and I'm not talking about the sophisticated (and expensive) wines that are now being made there by more experimental winemakers, but jugs of cloying stuff that tasted like strawberry jam mixed with a little paint thinner. But it's easy to make converts, and I have yet to find someone who actively dislikes a bottle of well-made sweet wine. In fact, I've discovered a surprising phenomenon while writing this book: While tasting, photographing, and experimenting with sweet wine and food combinations, there were many occasions when I sipped sweet wine for most of the day. When my assistant and I stopped for lunch, we used to open a bottle of dry wine to give ourselves a break, but discovered that our palates had so gotten used to the wine being sweet that the dry wine tasted harshly acidic and even metallic.

When I started writing this book, I naïvely thought I already knew a lot about sweet wines, since I'd tasted a good number of Sauternes, late-harvest German wines, and plenty of good port. But as I tasted and studied, I realized that I was dealing with an enormously complex subject and that sweet wines are made virtually every place where wine is made. So I must admit there are woeful lacunas—an understatement, since whole continents have been left out. I include not a single wine from South America; Washington and Oregon are almost absent; and California is covered in a few pages when it really merits its own book.

In my defense, much of the problem has to do with arcane laws and the fact that wineries are not allowed to ship directly to buyers in New York State, which happens to be where I live. The result has been that I've had to buy whatever I could find in wine stores or by traveling to where the wine is made. Trips to Italy, France, and California have been helpful, but each place is so huge and so diverse that I could spend a year (or at least several months) traveling to the various winemaking regions.

So I must apologize to those hardworking winemakers I've left out, many of whom have taken a chance in making a sweet wine, an expensive and risky undertaking. Sweet wines are difficult to make because often the grapes must be harvested late in the season, increasing the risk of a rain- or hailstorm that can ruin the entire harvest. Some wines require multiple harvests of grape clusters or even of individual grapes that have withered or been attacked by the right kind of mold. Such methods are not always reliable, and they're certainly not cheap.

If it's any consolation, I hope to encourage people to enjoy at least some of the many sweet wines that are the fruit of so much toil. For these fickle and difficult-to-make wines are truly among the world's greatest and, sadly, the least appreciated. I sincerely hope this will change.

Writing Sweet Wines has been a fascinating and delicious adventure (I've been telling friends that I have the best job in the world and one of the few in which you're supposed to drink at work). Especially fascinating has been the history of sweet wines and how and when they were drunk. Nowadays most of us may drink a little wine before a meal (usually dinner) as an aperitif, during the meal, and occasionally after the meal, but in times past wine was drunk at all times of the day. In Victorian England, even the most humble households had a sideboard with a decanter or more of fortified wine such as sherry, usually served in the late morning; Madeira or Marsala for the afternoon; and port for after dinner. Sweet wines were also provided at various times during a meal, not just with dessert. It's easy to imagine the days before central heating, when a glass of strong wine would provide much welcome warmth. Even though we now rarely use wine to warm ourselves up, we often drink cocktails or dry wine before dinner, a habit to which sweet wines offer a novel and exciting alternative.

I hope that this simple primer will awaken you to myriad little-known wines, many of which, like great works of art, alter our experience and transform the simple acts of eating and drinking into a communion of the table.

Opposite: While drinking sweet wine such as this Ste-Croix-du-Mont with oysters may seem frightful, in the 19th century Sauternes was de rigueur whenever oysters were served. In fact, sweet wines, especially Sauternes and most typically Château d'Yquem, were often served with the fish course. I'm too great a fan of bone-dry wines with oysters to indulge in this combination very often, but the match is surprisingly good.

AN INTRODUCTION TO SWEET WINES

Unlike many foods and drinks, a good sweet wine is not an acquired taste—once sipped, it is immediately and often surprisingly appealing. But the habit of drinking sweet wine regularly and with savory foods—something I suggest throughout this book—takes a little practice. If you're just starting, order sweet wine in a restaurant that offers it by the glass or half bottle. Most sweet wines you'll probably want to try first with or as dessert, but others, such as sweet sherries, Madeira, and Australian muscats and tokays, will be more exciting with cheese, while relatively dry Mosel Kabinetts and Spätleses make such lovely aperitifs that you'll never want chardonnay again.

In this introductory section I give you some suggestions on how to taste and describe sweet wine, and I explain how it is made. I suggest you read this information first because it will help you understand the more detailed descriptions of the wines that come later in the book.

HOW TO TASTE WINE

Few events in day-to-day life bring about the consternation of going into an unknown wine store or opening a wine list in a French or Italian restaurant. I've been victim to these anxieties myself, desperate to get it right, and always anxious to look good in front of friends and wine stewards alike. I don't know what it is about wine that turns certain people into pretentious snobs, but we need to remember that wine is here to give us pleasure, nothing else.

In restaurants there's the nerve-racking little ritual of the waiter showing us the wine (be sure to look; it sometimes happens that they come out with something you didn't order) and then presenting us with the cork, which we're supposed to smell, though it always smells like what you'd think—a cork. When the sommelier or waiter opens our wine for us to taste, what are we supposed to do? Well, most of the time, nothing, except take a sip, wait a few seconds, take another sip, and, if all is well, nod. Of the hundreds of bottles I've drunk, I've sent back maybe a dozen. You shouldn't send a bottle of wine back because you don't like it; there must be something identifiably wrong with it, which is somewhat unusual. If you suspect something is amiss but you're not sure—your white wine is brown and smells like bad sherry (it's maderized) or your red wine smells like a cork (such wines are said to be "corked")—engage the waiter or whoever is in charge of the wine by saying, "I think blah blah blah, what do you think?" I've never had anyone refuse to take a wine back.

Once your wine is in the glass, remember that there's no right or wrong way to describe it. While there are certain objective qualities that people agree on, tasting wine happens in your own universe. And whether you're a beginner or have been drinking wine for years, it's your relationship and personal memory of the wine that you're concerned with—it's all how it tastes or smells to you. Now of course there are those among us who try to show off by identifying an unknown wine or by going on

about this or that characteristic, but most of the time we fall flat on our faces. The hardest thing about tasting wine is *remembering* what it tastes like, not tasting it.

But how to go about it? Well, first, you can learn a lot about wine by looking at it. White wines darken as they age and are typically more deeply colored if the grapes have been left on the vine a long time, as is often the case with sweet wines. Wine that's made in a fresh style—say a German or Alsatian riesling—may start out pale yellow or green and turn to orange or gold. Wine made in an oxidized style (aged in casks and allowed contact with heat and/or air), such as an Australian muscat, will be some hue of brown. If a dry white wine or a sweet wine that's supposed to be fresh and fruity is in fact brown, watch out—it may have oxidized in the bottle. If you're not sure—this happens to me when I don't know how the wine is *supposed* to look or taste—ask the wine steward or take the wine back to the store and ask the proprietor. Red wines change from deep purple to red to brick-colored as they age (hence the word *tawny* for certain aged ports). Remember that age is relative and that some wines will age to maturity in three years or less while others ripen only after 50 years. Remember also that the wine's absolute age is less important than its maturity. The color will tip you off before you even touch the glass.

After you've stared at the wine for a second or two, pick it up and smell it. Don't swirl it right away because it may have such a generous aroma that swirling will needlessly exaggerate it. If you can't smell anything, tilt the glass away from you for a second—this will expose more of the wine to air and magnify the smell. If you still can't smell much, give the glass a swirl. The aroma of wine tells you as much if not more about a wine than does its taste—winemaking is very much an olfactory art form. If you're conscientious and concentrate on the wine (provided, of course, the wine is complex enough to give you something worth smelling), you may smell all sorts of things, some of them odd and particular to your own experience: a certain tree in your backyard, the smell of a certain book, or often the smell of a certain food. You may recognize a familiar smell but have trouble putting your finger on it—frustrating, but fun when you finally get it. At first you might not smell much at all—it'll just smell like wine—but it's worth persisting. I use a mental checklist of families of aromas, such as spices, fruits, herbs, chemicals, vegetables, or wood, to help me explore. It helps to sniff with friends, because more often than not someone at the table will identify an aroma that, once voiced, becomes immediately obvious.

Other than recognizing very particular aromas, there are certain characteristics to look out for. You may smell sulfur—almost universally used in winemaking (actually sulfur dioxide gas, which smells like burning matches and justifies sending the bottle back). Notice also if you smell alcohol or fruit, or if there's anything moldy or dirty or unwinelike about the aroma. Do you smell only wood? Sometimes there are "off" aromas of mildew or unpleasant, gassy smells such as hydrogen sulfide, which smells like rotten eggs. Much of the time, small amounts of certain aromas will dissipate in the glass during the course of a meal.

When sniffing your wine, if you don't get very far at first, don't give up. Sip it awhile and come back to it. A complex wine will change over the course of a meal and may not come into its own until you've got a pitiful thimbleful left in your glass. Most of this is a result of changes in the wine itself, but it may also be that your nose fatigues to certain odors that dominated when you started tasting, only to reveal other, more subtle aromas you hadn't detected at the beginning.

When you've given the wine a good sniff, take a sip, wait ten seconds, and take another sip. The way wine tastes is relatively simple compared to the way it smells. Again, there's no right or wrong thing to taste, but there are certain characteristics to look out for. What do you taste first? Do you taste fruit? Is the wine tart? If it's a red wine, ask yourself if it makes your mouth pucker, a sign that the wine contains tannins that will help it age

and possibly signal that you opened the bottle too soon or need to drink it with food. Does the wine make your mouth feel hot? This is a sign that the wine may contain too much alcohol or may need to be colder. Is the taste of the wine consistent with the aroma? Sometimes a wine will have an opulent aroma only to disappoint once tasted. Notice the relationship between the things you taste so that you can ascertain if the wine is balanced: it's the relationship between various tastes such as fruit, alcohol, and acid (the tartness of the wine) that tells you if the wine is balanced. This may take a little practice, so don't worry too much about it; just make a mental note of those things you do notice.

At this point, it helps to talk about the wine with your tablemates and compare notes. I often learn a lot about wine from people I'm drinking with, especially beginners whose first impressions are unhampered by preconceptions about the wine. When you take your first sip of wine, notice what happens in your mouth. Does the flavor of the wine linger (a good thing) or does it immediately disappear? If the latter occurs, the wine is said to be "short." What is the taste left in your mouth immediately after you swallow the wine? Wine people often describe this taste as the "finish," a term that can be helpful when you're comparing notes such as "It has a taste of coffee in the finish." (All these terms and many more are explained in A Little Wine Vocabulary, page 6).

Keep in mind that the flavors and aromas of wine can be very subtle and difficult to classify even after a lifetime of drinking. Because many sweet wines last very well once opened, I've had the opportunity to taste some of the wines in this book over and over again only to have a completely different impression on the second, third, or fourth tasting. One trick that I find immensely helpful is to serve two or more wines at the same time. When dining in groups, we often order more than one bottle anyway, so try overlapping similar wines: you will find the differences are much easier to perceive when the wines are right next to each other. By drinking more than one wine at once, you can make a kind of game out of it, letting everyone pitch in with his or her ideas about the wines. When you and your friends have had a little practice, you may want to cover up the labels so no one will be prejudiced.

I heard a story about a famous wine writer who was asked if he ever made a really serious tasting mistake, such as confusing a Burgundy with a Bordeaux. His answer was "Not since lunch." So fear not.

WHAT MAKES SWEET WINE SWEET?

Wine is grape juice that yeasts have turned into wine by converting the sugar in the juice into carbon dioxide and alcohol. When the amount of alcohol in the wine reaches about 14% and occasionally higher, the yeasts drown in their own alcohol and can no longer live. The wine stops fermenting. Sweet wines are made by stopping the yeasts before they ferment all the sugar, leaving natural grape sugar in the wine. Most sweet wines are made in one or more of seven basic methods.

The most obvious way to make a sweet wine is to start with grapes that contain so much sugar the yeasts can't possibly ferment it all. Some grapes such as Pedro Ximénez, used to make an intensely sweet wine that in turn is used to sweeten dry sherry, contain so much sugar that the yeasts can stop fermenting and still leave plenty of sugar in the wine.

In some places, grapes are allowed to dry out into raisins—or into something between a raisin and a grape—so the sun concentrates their sugar, leaving more sugar in the grape juice than the yeasts are able to turn into alcohol. There are several ways to do this. The most basic is to leave the grapes on the vine, sometimes twisting the stems leading to the bunch and cutting off its water supply; as a result, much of the water in the grape evaporates and the grape sugar is concentrated. The French call grapes and wines that are treated in this way *passerillé*; in Italy they call them *passito*.

Another method, used to make *vin de paille*—literally "straw wine"—consists of drying ripe grapes on racks or straw sheets either in the sun or the shade, and sometimes both (see Vin de Paille, page 40). Italy makes the greatest number of dried grape wines, including the much appreciated vin santo, but dried grape wines are also made in France, Germany, and California. Many of these wines have been made for thousands of years using the same techniques.

When ripe grapes are left on the vine, they are sometimes attacked by a mold, *Botrytis cinerea*, often called "noble rot." Botrytis can ruin a vineyard's harvest by attacking the wrong kinds of grapes or by attacking them at the wrong time. But when conditions are right—sunny days with moist,

Many regions of France have their own *vin de liqueur*, made by adding brandy or other spirits to grape juice. Here is one way to appreciate the subtleties of a vin de liqueur—taste three at once (left to right): Château d'Arlay (a Macvin de Jura), Floc de Gascogne, and Pineau des Charentes.

Look for a balance of flavors, plenty of fruit from the grapes, nice complexity, and a long finish. Vins de liqueurs often taste and smell too much like alcohol or whatever spirit it was that was used to stop the fermentation—such as Cognac for Pineau des Charentes, young Armagnac for Floc de Gascogne, and marc (the French version of grappa) for Macvin du Jura. All of these wines have a delicate sweetness and acidity that keep them from seeming heavy. They often have the aroma of partially raisined grapes. All make great aperitifs.

foggy mornings—botrytis concentrates the grapes' natural sugar and acids and imparts an unmistakable butterscotch aroma and flavor to the grape juice and then the wine. Botrytis's usefulness was discovered in Hungary, Germany, and France in the 17th and 18th centuries. Many of the world's greatest sweet wines—Sauternes, the late-harvest rieslings of Germany, late-harvest chenin blanc from the Loire Valley, and Hungarian Tokaji—are made with botrytized grapes. Because botrytis doesn't attack all the grapes at once, harvesting the grapes may require several trips out to the vineyard. This explains why some wines such as Sauternes are so expensive.

Virtually any must—grape juice—can be converted to a sweet wine by adding pure alcohol or brandy to the wine before, during, or after fermentation. The added alcohol artificially increases the concentration of alcohol in the partially fermented juice, killing the yeasts and stopping the fermentation. When the alcohol is added will determine the amount of natural grape sugar left in the wine—the sooner the alcohol is added, the more natural sugar will remain. Wines to which alcohol is added are called fortified wines. Fortified wines such as Madeira, port, sherry, and Málaga are among the best-known sweet wines in the world. Fortified wines are often referred to by their French name, *vins doux naturels*.

While fortified wines are made by adding alcohol to the wine during or after fermentation, some sweet "wines"—what the French call *vins de liqueur* or *mistelles*—are made by adding alcohol to unfermented grape juice. If enough alcohol is added, the grape juice is preserved, and the resulting drink is sweet from the grapes and sufficiently alcoholic that it doesn't ferment. After more or less prolonged aging in casks, these wines—Pineau des Charentes may be the best known—are usually served cool as aperitifs.

Because yeasts need warmth to ferment grape juice, they can be chilled into inactivity by refrigerating the fermenting grape juice. Originally this happened naturally by fermenting the juice late in the season when the cellars were simply too cold to allow the yeasts to finish fermenting. Nowadays wines are often fermented in stainless-steel tanks equipped with refrigeration coils, which make it easy to closely regulate the temperature. When chilled, most of the dead yeasts fall to the bottom of the partially fermented wine and the wine can be siphoned off—a system called racking—leaving the wine perfectly clear and free of yeasts, which might otherwise ferment the wine once it's bottled. Sulfur, in the form of sulfur dioxide gas or powdered sulfur salts, is sometimes added at this point to kill the yeasts and stop fermentation. The fermenting wine can also be centrifuged to get the yeasts out and stop fermentation.

Ice wine—*Eiswein* in German—is made by leaving the grapes on the vine so late in the season that they freeze. The grapes are then quickly pressed: the frozen water is retained in the press, while the sugar and concentrated juices—which freeze at a lower temperature than water—come through to yield a very sweet grape juice. Traditionally most ice wines come from Germany, but great ones are also made in Canada and Austria. Some winemakers in California have made ice wines by freezing the grapes in large freezers. The results have been mixed. (See Eiswein, page 69.)

Some sweet wines are made by mixing an intensely sweet wine or wine must (the unfermented juice) with a dry wine. Blends of sherry such as cream sherry and sweet versions of oloroso and amontillado are made by combining very sweet wine made from Pedro Ximénez or muscat grapes with dry sherry. For less expensive wines, boiled down grape must is sometimes added to the finished wine to increase its sweetness.

These methods can be used in combination. For example, the grapes in an ice wine are often also attacked by botrytis, and the fermenting wine from botrytized grapes may be chilled at an exact stage in its fermentation to control the final alcohol and sweetness in the wine.

A LITTLE WINE VOCABULARY

Some of us get nervous talking about wine and will avoid much of the colorful and descriptive vocabulary out of fear of sounding pretentious. Just describe a wine as "complex" to someone who has no knowledge of wine and see the reaction you get. But while there's always the risk of sounding like a wine snob if you throw certain words around in the wrong company, wine terms make you think about wine in a systematic way and will eventually help you remember the flavor and aroma of individual wines and lead to a sound familiarity with what you are drinking. Here are a few definitions:

ACIDITY: All fruits, including grapes, contain acids that when present in small amounts impart a pleasant (and in wine, essential) tartness. Some wines—French Chablis and Muscadet come to mind—are both acidic and almost perfectly dry, traits that give these wines their crispness. Sweet wines require a lot of acidity to balance the sugar they contain. In fact, the sweeter the wine, the more acid is required to set off the sugar. Sweet wines that contain too little acid taste flat, cloying, and too sweet, and we tire of them quickly. If a wine—dry or sweet—contains too much acid, it will taste overly tart and perhaps harsh.

ALCOHOL: All wines contain alcohol. Alcohol is of course an essential part of what makes wine enjoyable because it relaxes us and increases our appetite. But alcohol is also essential to the way wine tastes and smells. A wine with too little alcohol may seem thin or cloying, and a wine with too much can smell hot—when you sniff it, you can actually feel the alcohol burning your nose. To some degree you can control the effect of alcohol on your nose and taste buds (if not on your brain) by adjusting the temperature of the wine. If a wine burns your nose, chill the wine slightly to keep the alcohol cold and less volatile. Sweet wines often contain more alcohol than regular table wines—which is part of the reason they're often served cold—but when all goes well, their complexity and generous fruit hold up to and balance the alcohol.

AROMA AND BOUQUET: If "nose" is a silly word for the way a wine smells, then what are "aroma" and "bouquet"? Aroma describes the smell of a young wine or a wine that simply smells of fruit. Bouquet describes an assortment—literally a bouquet—of smells of a mature wine that come about during aging. Many of these fragrances are esters, compounds responsible for the flavor and aroma of fruits. Esters generated in wine as it ages are created when acids in the wine combine with ethyl alcohol (the kind we drink), as well as with complex alcohols such as amyl and butyl alcohols. As wine ages, aromatic ethers are also produced when two alcohols—not necessarily different kinds—bind together.

AUSTERE: Wines that show great restraint are said to be "austere." An austere wine is not necessarily the opposite of a generous wine; an austere wine simply has a tighter structure with less apparent fruit. Some of the greatest wines in the world are austere. Austerity is less common in sweet wines than it is in dry wines. Many austere wines may smell of minerals, rocks, or cement rather than fruit. While drinking rocks may not sound particularly wonderful, the experience of an opulently sweet wine with the flavors and aromas of minerals is a very special one indeed. Some German wines and wines from France's Loire Valley share these characteristics.

BALANCE: While the combination of flavors and aroma in wine is infinitely complex (this is what makes drinking it such fun), the basic structure of wine is—with a little practice—relatively easy to assess. "Balance" refers to the interrelationship of the wine's basic building blocks of acid, alcohol, sugar, tannin (in red wines), wood, fruit, and aroma. When all these ingredients are in harmony, the wine is said to be balanced. A wine that's too acidic will taste overly tart, and a wine that's too sweet will taste cloying and monotonous. If a wine contains too much alcohol, it will burn your nose when you sniff it (this is why wines with too much alcohol are said to be hot); if a wine contains too little alcohol, it will taste thin. If a wine is dominated by the taste of wood, the delicate flavor of its fruit will be lost or compromised. When describing a wine's balance, remember that the absolute amount of each of the components isn't the issue—it's the relationship of the components with one another that counts.

BODY: A young wine with a lot of "body" has a full texture and fills your mouth with a single flavor of grapes and fruit; an old wine, with complex assorted flavors. A wine with little body may taste watery or thin.

BOTRYTIS: Often called noble rot (or, in French, pourriture noble), *Botrytis cinerea* is a mold that attacks grapes as they ripen and imparts a wonderful flavor of its own. Many sweet wines are made from grapes that have been affected by botrytis because botrytis concentrates both the sugar and the acid in the grapes, so that more sugar remains in the wine after fermentation. Botrytis also imparts a flavor reminiscent of butterscotch or honey.

BREATHING: Many of us know we're supposed to open a bottle of red wine an hour or two before serving to let it "breathe." It's true that exposure to air causes many of wine's aromas to volatilize—or "open up"—so we can smell them, but wine that's simply had the cork pulled out isn't going to breathe much, because very little of the wine is actually exposed to air. A better method is to pour the wine into another container, preferably one that will expose the wine to a goodly amount of air. Doing this, even 15 minutes ahead of time, will often work miracles—it's like putting the wine under a magnifying glass.

I use a decanter with a very wide base and a narrow neck, but even pouring half the wine into an empty wine bottle will help it aerate quickly and encourage it to release its aroma. (See also Decanting, page 12.)

BREEDING: "Breeding" is a good descriptive word as long as you use it to describe wine and not people. Only the finest and most exciting wines are said to have good breeding—a subtlety and reserve that work in harmony to give the wine its particular identity. Wines with breeding are also almost always complex.

CLOYING: Monotonous. Wine that's out of balance so that its flavor—usually too sweet, with too little acidity—is said to be "cloying." We quickly tire of drinking a wine that's cloying.

COMPLEX: There's nothing complex about complexity—complexity just means that there's a lot going on. A "complex" wine may defy description, since its aroma, bouquet, and flavor keep changing. The greatest wines often evoke images of things past and have perfumes so subtle that we don't have names for them. I've experienced wines that have literally dozens of aromas that take up to an hour of concentrated sipping to identify.

DRINKABLE: The attributes that make a wine impressive are not always what make it fun, easy to drink, and good with food. Wines that are low in alcohol, with crisp, good acidity, and that can be drunk in relatively large amounts without being overly intoxicating are said to be "drinkable." ("Drinkable" is not the opposite of "undrinkable.") Most sweet wines, because they're best enjoyed in relatively small amounts, are not described as drinkable. German rieslings, especially Kabinetts, Spätleses, and Ausleses, are an exception; because of their low alcohol content and sprightly acidity, they are among the most drinkable of all wines.

DRY: This is perhaps the most misused word to describe wine, because dryness is often confused with acidity. Dryness is the absence of sugar in a wine, not the presence of tartness, which is caused by acid. No sweet wine can be described as dry, but the *effect* of dryness is sometimes imparted by a large amount of natural acid.

DUMB: Sometimes you run out and buy a wine that you remember was marvelous six months ago only to find that it doesn't taste or smell like much anymore. Such wines are said to be "dumb" or to be going through a "dumb phase." Dumbness is the opposite of generosity and is sometimes the result of drinking a wine too young. Such wines are said to be "closed in." Young wines often have a full aroma and taste of fruit. After a year or so in the bottle, this fruitiness can disappear and the wine is described as dumb. The dumb phase may last a year or more before the wine matures and its flavor and aroma (and bouquet) blossom. If the wine is already opened, decanting can remedy this.

EISWEIN: German for "ice wine," which is made from frozen grapes. (See also Eiswein, page 69.)

ELEGANT: Usually used to describe wines whose elements are in harmony with one another. "Elegant" wines are usually fragrant and racy, complex without being heavy, cloying, or monotonous. Such wines have an identity all their own.

FADING: Decanting a young wine or opening the bottle allows the wine to breathe and its aroma to emerge. Older wines, however, can be harmed by being decanted or by being allowed to breathe too long. Because the bouquet of older wine is complex and volatile, it can actually evaporate. When this happens, the wine is said to have "faded." Fading can also happen in the glass.

FINISH: The "finish" is what's left in your mouth after you swallow. If the flavor of the wine lingers in your mouth for more than a few seconds, the wine has a "long finish." If the flavor immediately goes away, the wine is said to be "short" or to have a "short finish." A long finish in a young wine may indicate that the wine will improve greatly with age.

FLABBY: A wine that's overly fleshy, with immediately available fruit and not enough acid to give structure and backbone to the fruit, is said to be "flabby." Flabby wines are the opposite of steely. We tire quickly of flabby wines. Chilling a flabby wine is sometimes helpful.

FLESHY: The opposite of austere, "fleshy" wines have an immediately available fruit both in the nose and on the palate. When you drink a wine that is fleshy, your mouth fills with flavor. Wines that are overly fleshy—without enough acid to support their fruit and/or alcohol—are described as flabby.

FLINTY: Some very fine white wines have a distinct mineral smell and taste that may remind you of a stone being broken open with a sledgehammer. Most "flinty" wines are dry—French Chablis is a good example—but occasionally sweet wines can also be flinty. The best examples of this combination of tastes are from Germany, especially from the Mosel and even more so the Saar, a tributary of the Mosel. Alsatian rieslings often have a flinty quality in the nose that's so reminiscent of a dry wine it comes as a delightful surprise to take the first sip and discover that the wine is sweet.

FRUIT: Don't confuse "fruit" with "fruitiness." Fruitiness is usually a simple flavor and aroma of some recognizable fruit, such as raspberries and strawberries (Beaujolais) or concord grapes (Manischewitz). Fruit, on the other hand, refers to the basic body of the wine and the intensity of the natural fruit flavors of the grape. Fruit is often contrasted with oakiness or other wood flavors that are imparted by aging the wine in wooden barrels. A wine that's aged too long in wood or that's spent too much time in the bottle is sometimes said to have "lost its fruit" or "dried out." The aroma and flavor of fruit in great wines is often of fruits other than grapes that don't actually exist in nature—this is part of wine's magic.

GENEROUS: A wine that has a full aroma and flavor and is forthcoming on the palate is said to be "generous." A young wine is generous when you can taste and smell the aroma of fruit; an old wine is generous when it has matured and has a rich bouquet and a full flavor.

HARD: Sometimes you'll be drinking a glass of wine and find yourself at a loss to describe it because it doesn't seem to taste or smell like much. When this happens, the wine is said to be "hard." Sweet wines are rarely hard because they're usually full of fruit and give generously of their flavor and aroma. Hard wines often just need a little time in the glass or opened bottle to soften and "open up." Aging hard wines in wooden casks or in the bottle in your cellar can also soften them. You can also decant a hard wine to get it to open.

HOT: A wine is said to be "hot" when you can smell alcohol or when the alcohol even stings the inside of your nose. The problem of too much alcohol in the smell of a wine can often be counteracted by cooling the wine slightly. Remember that red sweet wines, such as port—or any wine, for that matter—should not be served at room temperature, but more at the temperature of a traditional wine cellar, between 55° and 60°F.

ICE WINE: Wine made from frozen grapes. (See also Eiswein, page 69.)

NERVOUS: Wine with a lively, crisp acidity that balances sweetness or flavors and aromas such as fruitiness. A wine that's "nervous" (in wine parlance, nervous is a compliment) keeps the palate fresh. The opposite of nervous is a wine that's out of balance without enough acidity, making it seem heavy, cloying, and flabby.

NOBLE ROT: See Botrytis.

NOSE: Just a funny way of saying smell, the "nose" is at least as important to a wine as its taste (actually, the two are inextricable).

PASSERILLÉ: Grapes that are left on the vine to dry out are said to be "passerillé." Such grapes have in general not been attacked by botrytis and produce wine with a raisinlike flavor.

PASSITO: An Italian word for wine that's been made from grapes that have been allowed to partially dry out—thus concentrating their sugar—either on the vine or on racks in the sun or shade.

RACY: Wines that are light, but not thin, and at the same time complex are said to be "racy." German rieslings and late-harvest Alsatian rieslings are racy because they have an edgy acidity matched with complicated fruit aromas. Racy wines are never heavy or monotonous.

RANCIO: Wine that is deliberately oxidized, usually in wooden casks, is said to develop "rancio." Some rancio wines are made using a solera system (see The Solera System, page 81) so that the style of the wine remains consistent over the years. To learn to recognize the style of a rancio wine, try tasting a vintage Maury next to a non-vintage version that has been aged in barrels in the sun.

RESIDUAL SUGAR: Sugar left in the wine after fermentation is called "residual sugar"; it is what determines how sweet the wine is. The relationship between the amount of sugar contained in the must—the unfermented grape juice—and the wine after fermentation determines the amount of alcohol in the wine (see Potential Alcohol and Residual Sugar, page 19).

RIPENESS: Because the ripeness of grapes has a profound effect on the flavor and aromas of the finished wine, the decision of when to pick the grapes is critical.

Ripening occurs when the acid in grape juice is converted into sugar and eventually, depending on how the wine is fermented, into more or less alcohol. If grapes are overripe, they'll contain enough sugar but may not contain enough acid, resulting in a wine that's flat tasting or even cloying. In some places, especially in the New World where the weather may be hot and dry, acid is added to the finished wine to balance the wine's sugar and alcohol. It is also important that grapes ripen slowly so they have time to develop flavor. Grapes that ripen too quickly—again sometimes a problem in the New World—will often produce a wine that lacks depth of flavor and complexity.

SHORT: When you sip a glass of wine and immediately notice its flavor, the flavor should linger in your mouth for at least several seconds. If you find yourself going "mmm" and then suddenly wondering "Where did it go?" the wine is "short." Wines that are short have little if any finish.

SMOOTH: This is a word often used by those who know little about wine and never used by those who do. It's somewhat meaningless when applied to wine but presumably suggests that no element in the wine—acid, alcohol, or tannin—dominates. Red wines with tannin have a distinctly rough texture in the mouth, often a sign of quality, but one that means that the wine needs more bottle age.

SOFT: A wine is "soft" when its flavors and aromas are easily accessible. A wine that's too soft—maybe it's spent too much time in oak barrels or it's made from overripe grapes—is sometimes said to be flabby or to lack structure. Soft wines often lack acid.

STEELY: Some of the world's great wines combine the aromas of fruit with a mineral aroma and taste that is sometimes described as "steely." Steely wines tend to come from northern climates and are made from grapes that haven't been allowed to ripen so much that they lose their tartness.

STRUCTURE: The basic components that make up wine—sugar, acid, tannin (in red wines), sometimes wood, and alcohol—are said to make up its "structure." All of these are independent of smell (the nose). Think of structure as the frame on which a wine's flavors and aromas are held.

SULFUR: Because sulfur—or actually, sulfur dioxide—is so useful, it's hard to imagine winemaking without it. It's used to sterilize equipment, ward off unwanted microbes, kill yeasts when they get carried away, and, when desired, to prevent a second fermentation called malolactic. Sulfur dioxide is produced by burning yellow sulfur and is perfect for winemaking since, when used judiciously, it doesn't stay in the wine. If too much sulfur is used, the wine will smell like burning matches or sting your nose. Bottle labels in the United States almost always mention that the wine contains sulfites, which are remnants of sulfur dioxide dissolved in the wine. For most of us this is harmless, but some people may develop a headache or other allergic reactions.

TARTRATE CRYSTALS: Many people panic when they see sediment in the bottom of their bottle of wine, sweet or otherwise. White sweet wines often have a sediment of shiny clear crystals that look like glass. These are tartrate crystals formed by the acid in the wine. Because they're harmless and taste-free, it's not worth bothering to decant white sweet wines just to get rid of them, although decanting is usually a good idea anyway.

TERROIR: Another one of those wine words that creates confusion, *terroir* literally means "soil" in French; *goût de terroir* is the soil's taste, something that doesn't sound pleasant at all. In fact, terroir doesn't mean the wine tastes like dirt, but rather that it has an identity that distinguishes it from similar wines, even those made close by and from the same kind of grapes. It is because of terroir that the labeling systems for so many wines are as specific as they are, sometimes identifying vineyards no larger than a few acres. This is in part because the quality of a particular vineyard may justify vinifying its wines separately, so that each wine retains its identity by not losing its *goût de terroir*. The finer the wine you drink, the more likely it is to have a *goût de terroir*. Wine could be said to be composed of terroir and varietal character.

THIN: A "thin" wine leaves you wanting more flavor or aroma—in fact, a thin wine may taste watery. Thin wines sometimes have been diluted by rain during the harvest. They can also be the result of vinifying underripe grapes, leaving the grape juice low in sugar and the wine low on flavor. Grapes that ripen too quickly may not have enough time to develop flavor and will produce wines said to be "low on fruit" or thin.

VARIETAL CHARACTER: When the qualities of a particular grape come through in a wine, the wine is said to have "varietal character." Some grapes are so malleable (for example, pinot blanc) that they are more likely to transmit flavors that are characteristic of a particular place (sometimes called *terroir*) or vintage. Other grapes, such as gewürztraminer, have so much character of their own that they are easy to identify. Varietal character is neither bad nor good, but often wines with an understated varietal character go better with food. The finest wines have both varietal character and *goût de terroir*.

VIN DE PAILLE: French for wine that has been made from partially dried-out grapes. Unlike a wine that's passerillé—made from grapes that have been allowed to turn to raisins on the vine—"vin de paille" is made from grapes that have been spread out on straw mats or racks to dry in the sun or in the shade of an attic. (See Vin de Paille, page 40.)

SWEET WINE STYLES

Sweet wines get their identity not only from the grapes used to make them, but from what's done to the grapes before, during, and after they ferment. Most wines, including most sweet wines, are protected from oxygen so they neither turn into vinegar nor oxidize. For some wines, especially sweet wines like certain sherries, Madeira, and the oxidized style of Banyuls and Maury, oxidation is encouraged by letting the wine come in contact with air or by leaving it in barrels or glass demijohns out in the sun. The aroma of these wines is sometimes described as *rancio*. If you want to taste the difference between a wine made in the rancio style and the same wine that's been protected from air and heat, compare a Mas Amiel 10- or 15-year-old cuvée with a Mas Amiel vintage.

Rancio-style wines are sometimes made using the solera system (see The Solera System, page 81), in which some of the older wine in a barrel is repeatedly drawn off and replaced with younger wine; over time, the barrel will come to contain many different vintages, giving the wine a consistent character. Some soleras, especially in the region of Jerez where sherry is made, date back to the 19th century. You can experience a similar difference in style by tasting a ruby and aged tawny port next to each other. The tawny may have spent as many as 20 years in cask (which lightens its color and turns it the color of brick), but unlike rancio-style wines, tawny port is kept cool during this aging. The ruby port is a much younger wine—some people prefer it because of its freshness—that has spent only two or three years in cask in the absence of air.

Other sweet-wine styles have to do with when the grapes are picked. If the grapes are picked too soon, they may not have enough sugar to produce sweet wine, and the juice may not have had enough time to develop flavor. This is the problem in hot climates, including some New World ones, in which the grapes ripen too quickly, leaving them little opportunity to develop character. If the grapes are picked too late, much of the acid in the wine, essential to the wine's structure, will be converted into sugar. The result will be a wine with too much alcohol (if the wine is allowed to ferment long enough) or too much sugar and not enough acid to balance the sweetness (if the fermentation is stopped earlier).

To experience two dramatic differences in winemaking style, taste a late-harvest German riesling—an Auslese or Beerenauslese—next to a late-harvest Alsatian riesling called a *vendange tardive* (see photograph on opposite page). The German example will contain much less alcohol because the fermentation is stopped before much of the sugar gets used up by the yeasts. In the Alsatian example, the wine will be fleshier and will contain more alcohol. Both should have plenty of acid to balance their sweetness. Next, try comparing a German wine from the Mosel with one from the Rheingau. The Rheingau usually has more expansive fruit and may be more luscious, while the Mosel will be leaner, with a streak of clean acidity running down the middle. If you put a New World riesling in the mix, you'll find that it's more like a Rheingau in style because the grapes will have gotten more sunshine than the grapes that grow along the banks of the Mosel—grapes that must struggle for survival in their very northern climate.

SERVING SWEET WINES

WHAT'S THE BEST SERVING TEMPERATURE?

Other than recognizing that most of us serve white wines too cold and red wines too warm, there's no hard and fast rule as to what serving temperature is best. I've horrified guests by sticking an opened bottle of port in the refrigerator for 15 minutes or so to cool it slightly, ideally to the temperature of a wine cellar, between 55° and 60°F. No wine is good served at the usual room temperature of 70°F.

Since most sweet wines are white, an ice bucket, refrigerator, or freezer are indispensable tools. Don't let wine sit in an ice bucket or freezer too long or it will lose fragrance and flavor and may taste austere or overly acidic. As a chilled wine warms, its acidity seems to decrease, and it becomes more aromatic; its alcohol may become more apparent (you'll both smell it and feel its heat in your nose), and its flavors and aromas are easier to recognize. I start out by thoroughly chilling a white sweet wine in an ice bucket or freezer and then leave it out while I'm drinking it so it warms both in the bottle and in the glass. If the wine tastes too acidic or austere, take it out of the bucket or freezer for a while; if it tastes flat or too sweet or smells alcoholic, put it back in the bucket, freezer, or fridge. Notice the change of flavors and smells as the wine warms in your glass. You may find yourself taking a wine in and out of the ice bucket several times—a great way to drive a waiter crazy— adjusting its temperature according to what it's doing.

DECANTING

Any well-made red wine and even some white wines release sediment as they age. If the bottle is stored on its side, this sediment forms in a line along the side of the bottle that was facing down; if the bottle has been stored upright, the sediment collects around the punt—the indentation in the bottom of the bottle. If you know a few days ahead of time that you'll be serving a bottle with sediment, set the bottle upright so the sediment falls to the bottom. If you're taken by a sudden whim and want to serve a bottle that's been stored on its side, handle the bottle gently, keeping it horizontal, with the line of sediment facing down so you don't disturb it. This is the original purpose of the wine baskets sometimes used by restaurants (now generally used for effect rather than utility). When opening a bottle on its side, angle the bottle upward just enough to keep the wine from pouring out.

To rid a wine of sediment, you need to decant it. Set up a desk lamp—restaurants use a candle because it's pretty, but a desk lamp works better—and gently pour the wine into a decanter with the light shining through the neck of the bottle. When you've decanted almost all the wine and you start to see sediment in the neck of the bottle, stop.

Decanting can also be used to accelerate a wine's breathing by exposing the wine to air and getting aromatic compounds in the wine to volatilize. Most sweet wines, both red and white, will benefit greatly from a few minutes to a few hours spent in a decanter. A decanter filled with golden wine creates a lovely effect.

WHAT ARE THE BEST GLASSES?

Other than holding the wine, glasses have two functions: to allow you to smell the wine at its best and to make it look its most elegant. Many people think they have to serve sweet wines in small glasses, probably because sweet wines are rich and we drink less of them at a sitting. But too small a glass leaves no room for the aroma to collect, and most of the wine's intrigue will, along with its smell, be lost.

My own favorite glass for sweet wines contains about 6 ounces, flares out at the bottom, and tapers in slightly at the top. I never pour more than 2 or 3 fluid ounces, so there's plenty of room for the wine's volatile aromatic compounds—its aroma—to concentrate. Red sweet wines, because they're served closer to room temperature, are a bit trickier. Most sweet wines contain a relatively high percentage of alcohol, and unless the wine

Below is a Wehlener Sonnenuhr Auslese, a Mosel (left), next to a late-harvest (*vendange tardive*) Alsatian riesling. The German wine has a citruslike aroma, a crisp acidity, and a little spritz and sweetness. The Alsatian version smells more like apples or pears, and what it lacks in delicacy it makes up for in robustness. Like the German wine, it has a little sweetness but more alcohol, making it more suited to food than the German, which would be better served alone as an aperitif. I cannot say that one of these wines is better than the other.

is cool, the smell and burning sensation can be too aggressive if the wine is served in too big a glass. If I'm unsure, I give the wine a sniff and a taste in one of my largest glasses—they hold 10 fluid ounces and are the same shape as my smaller glasses. If it smells hot, of alcohol, or it burns my nose, it's either too warm or the glass is too big.

If I'm serving a special wine, red or otherwise, I use the biggest glass I can find to capture the wine's aroma. The only exception to this is when I'm serving wine that's very alcoholic—as are many fortified wines—and I want the aroma of alcohol to be muted. Certain wines are so old and/or rare that we may want to serve them by the thimbleful. If you serve such a wine in a large glass, a good percentage of it will end up clinging to the inside of the glass. For these wines, I use smaller—at times very small—glasses.

Wineglasses should be pretty to look at. Look for the simplest design—any superfluity subtracts from the beauty of the wine—and the thinnest glass you can afford. Unless you're having a big party and don't want to use your best glasses, avoid glasses with a thick rim around the top. Don't ever use colored glasses; they distract from the wine. Don't feel obliged to always use stemware. Glasses without stems, provided they have ample room to collect the wine's aroma, have an appeal all their own. When using stemmed glasses, hold the glass by the stem so you don't warm the wine.

HOW MUCH TO SERVE?

Since very few sweet wines could be called cheap, and indeed some are so expensive that the wine store may as well offer to gift wrap them, it's helpful to have some validation. First, because sweet wines are very rich and usually more intensely flavored than dry wines, you can get by serving very little—as little as an ounce per person, an amount that gives you 12 servings from a half bottle. The other great thing is that many sweet wines,

especially whites, keep well in the refrigerator once opened, especially if you top them off with inert gas (see page 113). So if you're stuck buying a whole bottle for a few guests or maybe just for yourself, it's helpful to know that you can keep most sweet wines for two weeks or even longer in the refrigerator without the wine perceptibly changing. I like to keep a collection of three or more white sweet wines on hand so I can serve guests more than one at a time, resulting in a little wine tasting that most people find surprising and fascinating.

Because red sweet wines, including vintage port, sweet Rasteau, and late-harvest zinfandel (or its cousin primitivo), are more susceptible to oxidation once opened than are whites, they are best drunk within a few days. Vintage port, like dry red wine, should be drunk all at one sitting unless, again, you top it off with inert gas. Oxidized-style wines such as Australian muscat and tokay, Portuguese Moscatel de Setúbal, Madeira, tawny port, sweet sherries, and Málaga are meant to be served over a period as long as several months and are usually bottled with a small twist-off cork, designed to be used again and again.

WHAT WINES GO WITH WHAT?

It's a pity that something as pleasurable as drinking wine becomes intimidating the minute many of us walk into a wine store. Of all the questions surrounding wine, the most confusing is deciding what wine to serve with what. Fortunately, it's very hard to go completely wrong, and most of us have enough common sense to avoid really disastrous combinations such as port with oysters. The most common mistake is serving an overly delicate wine with robust food, so you don't taste the wine. While there are certain wine and food pairings that are made in heaven, much of the time these are serendipitous and difficult to predict, a result of the perfect wine from the perfect vintage at just the right age with just the right food. It's better to keep in mind a few rules and possible approaches instead of conducting a frustrating search for the happy coincidence.

Sweet wines are often mismatched with food because most of us think that sweet wines are *dessert* wines. True, sweet wines can make a delicious after-dinner treat, but they are often the least dramatic at the end of a meal when your palate is tired, and especially when the wine is asked to compete with an overly sweet dessert. The wine should always be sweeter than the dessert; if it isn't, the wine will taste harsh and overly acidic, and any rich lusciousness it may have will go unappreciated. If you want to serve a sweet wine at the end of a dinner, play it safe—serve it with one of the desserts in this book, serve it with a pear, or serve it with something savory like a wedge of aged hard cheese or a few nuts. Many of us make the mistake of looking for similar flavors in a wine and the food it's paired with. Remember that wine can also be used to provide contrast. If the same flavors occur in both the food and the wine, they'll cancel each other out, and while the combination won't be bad, it will lack the interplay of opposites that makes drinking wine with food so interesting.

Sweet wines are often at their dramatic best *before* dinner, as an aperitif. This makes a lot more sense than serving a glass of chardonnay or even red wine, because those wines are designed to go with food. Because sweet wine served before dinner, maybe with a little hors d'oeuvre like a few nuts or olives, will create an immediate impact, it's a time to serve some of your best wines—wines you don't want ignored come dessert, when everyone is sated with both drink and food. One approach worth trying, whether at home or in a restaurant, is to order (or bring out) a bottle of sweet wine and drink half of it as an aperitif and, when appropriate, with the first course, and save the second half to drink at the end of the meal, with or without dessert.

A surprising number of sweet wines are best served with savory foods. This makes sense when you think about it, since sweet and savory balance each other. I often serve a moderately sweet wine with a first course of

seafood, such as the Braised Sea Scallops with Saffron on page 27, or with something containing cheese such as the Goat Cheese Soufflés on page 100. Try serving sweet wines in order of ascending sweetness—perhaps a German Mosel as an aperitif and a late-harvest Vouvray *moelleux* (sweet) or an Alsatian *vendange tardive* with the first course—and I guarantee your guests will be thrilled. This strategy is also a good one when you're serving champagne or cocktails with hors d'oeuvres. If you try following champagne or cocktails with a dry white wine, the wine will taste flat. A sweet wine, on the other hand, will taste fresh and exciting and will catch everyone delightfully off guard. What comes as the biggest surprise is the affinity of sweet wines, even white wines, to robust-flavored foods, including those made with red wine. The Oxtails Braised in Banyuls recipe on page 42 is great with late-harvest riesling from Alsace, California, or Germany's Rheingau or Rheinpfalz.

While it hasn't occurred to many of us to serve sweet wines before a meal, there is one family of sweet wines that has long been appreciated as an aperitif. So-called *vins de liqueur* are wines that in a sense aren't really wines at all because the grape juice is never allowed to ferment. Instead, spirits such as Cognac (added to make Pineau des Charentes) or Armagnac (added to make Floc de Gascogne) are added to the freshly pressed grape juice to preserve the natural fruitiness and sweetness of the juice. Vins de liqueur can be served chilled or, scandal of scandals, on the rocks, but avoid the ice cubes, if not the chilling, when serving a more expensive bottle.

Sweet wines are magnificent with cheese, especially hard and aged cheeses like English cheddar and aged Gouda, blue cheese such as Roquefort and Gorgonzola, and some goat cheeses. I serve cheese either French style, after the main course, maybe with a little fruit; or in the American way, as an hors d'oeuvre. Foods made with cheese such as soufflés or grilled cheese sandwiches can find no better match than a sweet wine, preferably one with a nutty style such as a moscatel sherry or an Australian muscat. Aged goat cheeses go especially well with wines made from chenin blanc, such as a Vouvray moelleux or demi-sec and a California late-harvest version.

Because most people know so little about sweet wines and are so amazed when they taste a good one, I sometimes turn dinner into a wine tasting of sorts by serving more than one sweet wine at once. Depending on the sophistication of your guests, you can pair more or less distantly related wines so people can easily perceive their differences. For a cheese course, for example, I might serve a botrytized semillon from Australia at the same time as a Sauternes or one of the Sauternes-like wines from nearby villages such as Ste-Croix-du-Mont and Loupiac and let my guests see the dramatic differences in color, flavor, and concentration. Good blue cheese is infallible with sweet red wines such as port, Banyuls, late-harvest Rasteau, or Italian late-harvest primitivo—the Italian cousin of zinfandel. Again, I might choose to serve two or more red sweet wines and explain a little about them to my guests, but allow the guests to discover the wines' nuances for themselves. Try serving,

for example, a glass of primitivo next to a glass of late-harvest zinfandel, or a glass of California port-style wine next to a port from Portugal.

Unlike many sweet wines that are moderately or only slightly sweet, intensely sweet wines are in fact best served after dinner: when served earlier in the meal, they overwhelm the palate and make both wine and food that follow taste too acidic or even bland. If you have a very special wine, perhaps a great Sauternes or a German *Trockenbeerenauslese*, you may want to organize the meal so that your palate isn't assaulted with too many rich or strong-flavored dishes. In situations like these, keep the meal simple and the wines leading up to the sweet wine dry, so the palate doesn't fatigue too early to sweetness. With the best and most expensive wines, I serve a piece of mild cheese, perhaps a ripe pear, or a not-too-sweet dessert such as the Blanc-mange on page 28 or the Hazelnut Biscotti on page 54.

Keep in mind that during the course of a meal wines should increase in sweetness, complexity, and age. If you serve a wine that's too sweet or just too luscious and complex, any wine that follows it—unless it's even greater—will be upstaged. If you're trying to show off a particular wine, keep the other wines at the meal modest so the best wine stands out.

One almost clichéd wine-and-food pairing is dry gewürztraminer with spicy foods. For the most part, dry gewürztraminer, while distinctive, is simply too delicate to stand up to an onslaught of spicy or, even worse, hot, spicy foods. A sweet gewürztraminer from Alsace or California, on the other hand, is magnificent. Riesling from Alsace, California, and Australia is a beautiful match for spicy foods, but don't serve your best wine with spicy food because your palate won't perceive subtle nuances under the aggressive flavors of the food.

If you're stumped and can't figure out what to pair with what, don't panic but instead feel free to experiment, and remember that there are a lot of happy accidents out there waiting to happen. Keep in mind that wines and foods from the same place often make a good match. Otherwise, how many of us would think of serving a riesling with a pile of sausages and sauerkraut (a *choucroute garnie*), a combination of a dish and a wine, both from Alsace, that work beautifully together.

It's a pity that sweet wine is so rarely served with a first course, since it is often with the start of a meal that sweet wines show themselves at their best. The French serve Sauternes or Monbazillac with foie gras, but other combinations are unusual. A sweet wine that's not too sweet makes a perfect opening to the Braised Sea Scallops with Saffron on page 27 or the Chicken Liver Mousse on page 37. If you serve drinks or champagne before dinner, a dry white wine is going to taste acidic and flat when you first sit down—and if you don't want to go straight to a red, a more or less sweet wine is the perfect answer and will catch even jaded guests completely off guard.

When serving a dessert with a sweet wine, avoid chocolate (despite the claims of those who insist chocolate is good with port) and lots of cream; most important, don't use too much sugar. If you're serving a very sweet or chocolate dessert, serve a cheese course after the main course and choose your wine to go with that. Fruit desserts, provided they aren't too sweet, make the perfect foil for sweet wines. Don't ever serve a slightly sweet wine—such as a Vouvray demi-sec—with a dessert, but stick with very sweet wines such as Sauternes or a sauvignon blanc–semillon blend such as California's Dolce, which will hold up to the sugar.

FROM AGING TO RESIDUAL SUGAR

AGING: One reason that sweet wines may have been so popular in times past is their longevity, even when not tightly sealed with a cork. Sugar, alcohol, and acid all act as preservatives and allow wines to be shipped long distances, even in the poorly stoppered amphorae used by the ancient Greeks and Romans. Except for sweet wines that are appreciated for their freshness—Moscato d'Asti bubbles up to mind—almost all sweet

wines benefit from time spent in the bottle. While many sweet wines don't show themselves at their best for 20 or more years, they are still luscious and delicious in their youth. Some wines, usually those made in an oxidized style, such as Madeira, or muscats and tokays from Australia, have already been aged in cask and benefit little from more time spent in the bottle. In fact, the corks for some of these bottles are the twist-off kind, implying that the bottle can be opened and served at more than one sitting. Such corks aren't designed for wines that spend years aging in a cellar.

Because wine is exposed to more oxygen in a cask than it is in a bottle, many wines are aged in casks before they are bottled, which greatly steps up the aging and gives the wine a nutty, oxidized flavor. For some wines, the casks are left out in the sun, which accelerates the aging even more. The amount of air allowed in the barrel also influences the style of the wine, with more exposure to air causing more rapid oxidation. In Jerez, where sherry is made, space is left in the barrels to encourage the growth of flor, a kind of yeast that gives some sherry its characteristic flavor.

If you plan on aging wines—I think of mine as a vinous 401(k)—keep them on their sides in a cool, dark place that has only minimal changes in temperature. You can see the aging of white sweet wines by their change in color, from pale yellow or green to golden and—sometimes a good thing, sometimes not—to brown. To see the color of red wines before you pull the cork, hold the bottle up to the light and look at the bottle's base. Look through the glass to one side of the punt, the indentation in the bottom of the bottle.

The rate at which a wine ages depends on the wine, with some changing noticeably in a couple of years and others making no change for ten years or more. Red wines, such as vintage ports, change color from purple to ruby red, to brick red, and when too old, brown. I've had 80-year-old port that's still ruby red and full of fruit and bottles of lesser creatures that have turned brown and lifeless in five to eight years.

CHAPTALIZATION: If you pick up most books about wine, within five minutes you'll run into the word *chaptalization*. Chaptalization is the method in which sugar is added to unfermented grape juice to increase the eventual wine's alcohol content or, if the fermentation is stopped before all the sugar has been fermented, its sweetness. The original purpose of chaptalization was to make wine more stable—sugar and alcohol act as preservatives—and longer lasting, but the result is often a wine that's out of balance because it has too much alcohol to properly match the fruit it contains.

Chaptalization is also sometimes used to make up for grapes that never ripened. Unripe grapes not only lack the sugar needed to make the wine sweet and provide it with enough alcohol, but they also haven't had enough time to develop flavor. Wines that have been chaptalized may taste or smell too strongly of alcohol. Purists frown on chaptalization, especially for sweet wines, because traditionally the sweetness in sweet wine should come from the grape itself. Occasionally you may run into the word *enrichment*, which is just a fancy way of saying chaptalization, except that wines are chaptalized with sugar, whereas enriched wines may have had concentrated grape juice added to the must (the unfermented juice) instead. Unfortunately, chaptalization is common even in places where it is illegal.

YIELDS: Wine writers are always talking about yields, the amount of wine produced from a given area of vineyard. It's been known for centuries that the fewer grapes a vine produces, the more concentrated the wine will be. Most countries in Europe have strict laws dictating the maximum yield a vineyard must produce to be entitled to use a specific name. European yields are usually expressed in hectoliters per hectare, which works out to about 10.7 gallons per acre if the yield were one hectoliter per hectare. Actual yields, however, are much greater. The average yield in Europe is about 50 hectoliters per hectare (535 gallons per acre), but for sweet wines yields are generally much lower because the grapes have often been shrunk by botrytis or have been left on the vine or in an attic to dry out. The low yield explains why so many sweet wines are expensive. Château d'Yquem produces a maximum of 9 hectoliters per hectare (96 gallons per acre), while most Sauternes are allowed to produce up to 25 hectoliters per hectare (267 gallons per acre), which is still much lower than most dry wines, even very expensive ones.

To complicate matters, in the New World yields are measured in tons (usually metric, but not always) of grapes per hectare or acre. Don't assume that these yield measurements can easily be converted into hectoliters per hectare: different grapes produce different amounts of juice. For particularly juicy grapes or grapes that are being used to make red wines—meaning that they are sometimes pressed harder to extract the red color—the winemaker may get 100 liters (106 quarts) of wine from 130 kilos (287 pounds) of grapes. Pressing too hard, however, can make a wine bitter. Making sweet wines is harder because the grapes have more often than not turned into raisins (imagine juicing a raisin), have withered with mold, or have frozen on the vine.

In general, the more specific the area described on the label is, the lower the permitted yield will be. For example, vines from the Coteaux du Layon along France's Loire Valley must not produce more than 35 hectoliters per hectare (374 gallons per acre) to legally have the words *Coteaux du Layon* on the bottle. If the winemaker also wants to include one of the approved village names along with the words *Coteaux du Layon*, his or her vines are allowed to produce only 30 hectoliters per hectare (321 gallons per acre). If the village happens to be the renowned village of Chaume, the maximum legal yield drops to 25 hectoliters per hectare (267 gallons per acre). If the wine is from the famous vineyard of Quarts de Chaume, the winemaker can put these words on the label with no mention of the Coteaux du Layon, but the vines will be allowed to produce only 23 hectoliters per hectare (246 gallons per acre).

POTENTIAL ALCOHOL AND RESIDUAL SUGAR: The sugar contained in unfermented grape juice is often expressed in terms of potential alcohol, the percentage of alcohol the wine would have if all the sugar were fermented. For example, in one system, if a sweet wine contains 12% alcohol and 8% residual sugar, the wine is said to have 20% potential alcohol. In a perfectly dry wine, potential alcohol and actual alcohol are the same. Much of the time, must (the unfermented juice) destined for sweet wine contains so much sugar that the yeast can't possibly ferment it all. Most yeast dies in an environment containing more than 14% alcohol, although certain powerful strains can ferment wine up to 17% alcohol. If fermentation is stopped by adding alcohol (fortifying the wine), juice with relatively low potential alcohol can still produce a sweet wine. If for example must has 14% potential alcohol but the fermentation is stopped when the wine reaches 7% alcohol, then the wine will have 7% residual sugar.

To complicate matters, there are several systems used to calculate the amount of sugar and thus the potential alcohol contained in grape juice. The Baumé system, popular in Europe, makes the most sense since it's calibrated on potential alcohol. So if grape juice has 10% sugar using the Baumé system, the juice will have a potential alcohol of 10%. In other words, if the wine is fermented until all the sugar is used up and the wine is dry, the wine will have 10% alcohol. In America winemakers are more likely to use the Brix system, which is based on the weight of dissolved matter (most of which is sugar) in the must. One degree Brix equals 18 grams per liter of sugar. Since it takes 16.5 grams of sugar to produce a dry wine with 1% alcohol, a must with 10 degrees Brix (the equivalent of 10.9 degrees Baumé) will produce a dry wine with 10.9% alcohol.

The amount of sugar left in the wine after fermentation is described as residual sugar, usually expressed as grams per liter. Almost all wines contain some residual sugar, and even the driest wines may contain as much as 2 grams—about half a teaspoon—per liter. If a wine contains a lot of acid, it can contain up to 25 grams per liter (about an ounce per quart) of residual sugar and still give the impression of dryness. Sweet wines vary enormously in the amount of residual sugar they contain, anywhere from 25 grams per liter to astonishingly high levels—around 600 grams per liter (more than a pound per quart!) for Tokaji Eszencia. When sugar in wine ferments, it takes 16.5 grams per liter (about a half ounce per quart) to produce wine with 1% alcohol. If a particular grape juice contains 500 grams of sugar per liter, it's said to have 25% potential alcohol. If it's then allowed to ferment to 13% alcohol, the wine will have 12% (120 grams per liter) residual sugar.

While you may have trouble making use of this information at first, more and more winemakers are starting to put it on the label—a big help in predicting the style of the wine and how best to serve it.

THE WINES

When researching wines for this book, I made the disconcerting discovery that virtually every country I surveyed produces such an interesting array of sweet wines, each place could warrant a whole book. In paring down a plethora of good wines and information about them, I've inevitably committed injustices. For one, I have listed the wines according to the country where they are made and haven't paid much attention to which wines are listed before others. For instance, French wines are covered first, which is not to say that they are better than all the others; however, because France makes so many different styles of sweet wines, in so many different regions, French wines can be used as a point of reference for wines made all over the world.

I've purposely avoided recommending specific wine and food combinations, and the recipes are sprinkled throughout the book so as not to imply that a particular dish has to be paired with exactly the right wine. I've been lucky to try many of these wines over and over again, with everything from Dover sole meunière to take-out pastrami sandwiches, and I've yet to come up with a combination that's truly bad. More often than not, I've discovered combinations that are surprisingly good. I have, however, consistently noticed one thing: because sweet wines are most often rich, a single glass is usually just right for a simple meal or a single course.

France

When it comes to drinking, the French are a versatile lot. While the Italians drink more wine, the French consume more alcohol because they drink it in myriad forms—from beer to wine to spirits. Fortunately for wine drinkers, this versatility extends to wines, both sweet and dry. French sweet wines come in all styles, from rich, golden Sauternes to delicate, late-harvest wines from Alsace and the Loire Valley. In the south we find port-like Banyuls and intensely floral Muscat de Beaumes-de-Venise. In eastern France we encounter exotic *vin de paille* made by drying the grapes on straw mats before they are turned into wine.

Many of France's sweet wines are so underappreciated that they are often a good value, and because of their diversity, there's at least one French sweet wine you can pair with each point in a meal or sip on its own as an aperitif, dessert, or after-dinner drink.

SAUTERNES AND BARSAC

For anyone who associates Sauternes with the cloying sweet wine sold in gallon jugs and labeled sauterne (not Sauternes), the first sip of authentic Sauternes is a revelation. With the possible exception of port, Sauternes is justifiably the world's best-known sweet wine. Sauternes is rich and luscious, with the flavor of honey, peaches, spices, butterscotch, and apricots and an intense sweetness balanced by generous acidity and a backdrop of subtle bitterness. Because it's so sweet, Sauternes is best served at dessert, if not as the dessert itself. Sauternes is so full-flavored and satisfying that an actual dessert is often superfluous. Sauternes should be served cold in large glasses to show off its golden color and to concentrate its complex aroma.

The word *Sauternes* is actually used to describe an area that includes five communes of which Sauternes is only one. Sauternes is a small town about 30 miles south of Bordeaux on France's Atlantic coast and is sur-

---

FIRST GREAT GROWTH
(PREMIER GRAND CRU)

Château d'Yquem

FIRST GROWTHS
(PREMIERS CRUS)

Château La Tour Blanche
Château Lafaurie-Peyraguey
Clos Haut-Peyraguey
Château de Rayne-Vigneau
Château Suduiraut
Château Coutet
Château Climens
Château Guiraud
Château Rieussec
Château Rabaud-Promis
Château Sigalas Rabaud

SECOND GROWTHS
(DEUXIÈMES CRUS)

Château Myrat
Chateau Doisy Daëne
Château Doisy-Dubroca
Château Doisy-Védrines
Château D'Arche
Château Filhot
Château Broustet
Château Nairac
Château Caillou
Château Suau
Château de Malle
Château Romer
Château Lamothe

rounded by lesser known towns where wine is made in the same way. Wine labeled Sauternes or Barsac (one of the nearby towns) must be made with sémillon and sauvignon blanc grapes that have been attacked by noble rot (botrytis), producing a wine with rich flavors and an intense aroma. Well-made Sauternes lasts for many years in the bottle—I envy a friend who once tasted an 1840 Château d'Yquem—but these days we rarely have the patience to wait the minimum of 20 years for the best Sauternes to mature.

Like many of the world's great late-harvest wines, the grapes for Sauternes are harvested more than once—usually about three times but as many as 11—so that only those grapes attacked by noble rot are used in the wine. At some châteaux, the last harvest occurs as late as November, a scary time because a sudden burst of rain or hail can ruin many of the grapes. Because grapes in the same vineyard are attacked by botrytis at different times, harvesting the grapes for Château d'Yquem and other Sauternes requires many trips—called *tries*—out into the vineyard.

The legendary wine made at Château d'Yquem is considered by some to be the greatest wine in the world. Needless to say, Château d'Yquem is expensive, but as the wine writer Gerald Asher once explained, a half bottle costs less than a pair of good football tickets.

Yquem's quality comes not only from perfect soil and climate, but from the infinite care taken in tending the vines and making the wine. The soil at Yquem is still tilled with horses, and all the grapes are harvested, sometimes one berry at a time, by hand. Château d'Yquem holds up for years—sometimes longer than a century—in the bottle, but it should be aged at least 20 years before being opened.

The production of Sauternes is closely controlled by the French government. Like red Bordeaux, almost all Sauternes are labeled with the name of a particular château. These châteaux are rated so that each falls into one of four categories: first great growth (*Premier Grand Cru*), first growth (*Premier Cru*), second growth (*Deuxième Cru*), and a large number of less prestigious châteaux. Thirteen Sauternes are second growths, 11 are first growths, and only one—Château d'Yquem—is a first great growth. Opposite is a list, first compiled in 1855, of the greatest Sauternes châteaux. Three great Sauternes—Château de Fargues, Château Gilette, and Château Raymond-Lafon—were left out, even though their quality matches many of those classified as first growths. Château de Fargues is particularly special. It is made by the owners of Yquem and has a similar style. While never cheap, it can be had for half the price of Château d'Yquem.

VILLAGES AROUND SAUTERNES

It wasn't until recently that Sauternes, after decades of being largely ignored, again became popular. The result is an improvement in its quality because the winemaker can charge enough for the wine to afford the great care needed to make it at its best. The downside, of course, is that Sauternes has gotten expensive. We can take some consolation in the fact that a little bit goes a long way—a half bottle is fine for six servings.

BLACK TRUFFLE CUSTARDS

I got the idea for this dish from the white truffle custards served at Thomas Keller's restaurant, The French Laundry, in Yountville, California. These custards are baked in the eggs' shells, meaning you'll need egg cups and small coffee spoons. You can also prepare them in 3- or 4-ounce ramekins. I serve these custards as a first course with a glass of Monbazillac, Sauternes, or late-harvest Alsatian riesling.

Makes 6 small but rich first-course servings

6 **large eggs** (save the carton)
1 **cup heavy cream**
1 **black winter truffle** (a small one is sufficient), chopped
    fine just before using
½ **teaspoon salt**
3 **grinds of fresh pepper**

Cut the tops off the more rounded end's of the eggs with an egg cutter, or by slicing slowly and carefully with a serrated knife, and discard the tops. Pour out the eggs, saving 4 egg yolks for the truffle custards (you can save the rest of the eggs for an omelet). Beat together the egg yolks and cream—don't overdo it or you'll whip the cream—and pour the mixture through a strainer. Stir in the chopped truffle, salt, and pepper. Rinse out the egg shells.

Preheat the oven to 275°F. Put the lower half of the egg carton in a baking dish and set the egg shells in the egg receptacles. Use a small ladle or a turkey baster to fill the egg shells about ¾ full with the custard mixture—be sure each one gets its fair share of truffle. Fill the baking dish with enough hot tap water to come halfway up the sides of the carton, cover the dish with aluminum foil, and bake for 45 minutes to an hour. Check that the custards are done by wiggling each one and making sure the custard doesn't slosh around too much. It's all right if the custard remains liquid, but it should be thick and unctuous. Serve the custards in egg cups. Give everyone a small spoon.

There are several villages near Sauternes and Barsac where Sauternes-like wines are made, and while these wines rarely have the richness of great Sauternes, they come close, and they're half the price or even less. Look for wines from Cérons, a village just northwest of Sauternes. Most of the wine from Cérons is vinified dry and sold as Graves, but with today's greater interest in sweet wines, a few vintners are again making sweet versions that rival good Sauternes. Wines from Loupiac are also hard to find, and when you do come across them, many are on the light side; but again, a few serious winemakers are putting energy into sweet versions. Ste-Croix-du-Mont and Cadillac wines are little known, but good ones can be fantastic—they sometimes have a nervous edge and a citrus aroma that Sauternes lacks.

All these wines have a distinct quality of their own and are well worth exploring. I serve them with blue and hard cheeses, Blanc-mange (see recipe, page 28), not-too-sweet fruit tarts, or in the afternoon, with a few cookies or Madeleines (see recipe, page 33) My favorite makers are: Château de Cérons (Cérons); Château La Grave, Château La Rame, Château Crabitan-Bellevue (Ste-Croix-du-Mont); Château Redon, Château Manos (Cadillac), and Domaine du Noble (Loupiac).

THE LOIRE VALLEY

The Loire is the longest river in France, and wine grapes grow along its entire length. The upstream half is mostly planted in sauvignon blanc, which is used to make dry wines such as Sancerre, and in lesser amounts in cabernet franc, which is used to make the delicious red wines Chinon and Bourgueil. Farther downstream, chenin blanc takes over, almost all the way to Brittany, where bone-dry Muscadet (no relation to muscat) is made. Starting around the city of Tours, some of the most delicious wines in the world are made. Best-known is Vouvray, but to the east, near the city of Angers, is the region of the Coteaux du Layon, known for its magnificent sweet wines. Within the Coteaux du Layon are even more special appellations and vineyards such as Bonnezeaux or Quarts de Chaume. Sweet wines of the Loire can often be found at bargain prices.

VOUVRAY

I once toured the Loire Valley on a tiny motor scooter meant for getting around Paris but no farther. The scooter eventually gave out from exhaustion, but I got a close look at rural France at its most beautiful. I remember one day in particular when I sat on the banks of the Loire looking at Chenonceaux,

SWEET WINE TASTINGS

One of the pleasures of writing about sweet wine is having a refrigerator full of various bottles and serving them casually to friends who drop by. It never fails to please when I make a little wine lesson out of it, pulling out maybe five or six wines made from the same grape or in the same place and letting my guests compare. I give very little wine—a couple of tablespoons per wine—so the wines last a long time and we can keep tasting until everyone is sated.

Some days, when I'm feeling particularly generous, I'll do more than one tasting—perhaps four different chenin blancs, then rieslings from around the world, then Sauternes and Australian liqueur wines, and if I'm going all out, a sip of 1834 Madeira or some Tokaji Eszencia. I put a little pitcher of water on the table so everyone can stand around, use the same glass for each wine, and chat. You don't have to be as extravagant as I am—two modest wines give people plenty to talk about.

COULÉE DE SERRANT

Years ago I read in a book by the famous French chef Ferdinand Point that in his opinion, the three greatest white wines in the world were Montrachet, Château d'Yquem, and Coulée de Serrant. Coulée de What? Today few people, even those who spend an inordinate amount of time and money learning about wines, have ever heard of this magnificent vineyard.

Coulée de Serrant is a 17-acre parcel of land in the Savennières region that in the 19th century and for centuries before produced some of the most renowned sweet wines. After years of going fallow, the vineyard was bought by a French surgeon, Nicolas Joly, who went about growing chenin blanc—the only grape permitted—following an 18th-century system called *biodynamisme*. Biodynamically grown grapes are tended not only according to the seasons but to the movement of the moon and planets. No fertilizers or insecticides are used.

The vineyard is now back in full form, but again, as is true for most of the wines of Savennières, it produces only dry wine. But Monsieur Joly has been toying with the idea of making a late-harvest sweet wine—a vin liquoreux. While the wines of Coulée de Serrant and Savennières are truly great and only moderately expensive, there is one drawback—they require at least 25 years to show themselves at their best.

the gorgeous château that skirts the river, while sipping a local Vouvray with my picnic of cheese and fruit.

One of the great underrated wines of the world, Vouvray is made near Tours, along the Loire's middle section. Vouvray must be made exclusively from chenin blanc grapes and is sold in three or sometimes even four levels of sweetness. Dry Vouvray is labeled sec and can be almost steely like a Sancerre. Lightly sweet Vouvray is labeled demi-sec, and because it is indeed only lightly sweet, it goes marvelously well with savory foods, especially the Fresh Morels with Cream on page 30. As Vouvray gets sweeter—and suddenly expensive—it is *moelleux*, made from withered bunches of grapes harvested late in the year. Intensely sweet and hard-to-find Vouvray made from individual botrytized grapes is labeled *liquoreux* or, by one maker, *moelleux réserve*. Sweet Vouvray wines—anything sweeter than demi-sec—are some of the hardest in the world to produce; in fact, they're only made in the best years, because Vouvray is so far to the north. To make a successful sweet Vouvray, the vineyard has to be harvested in stages so only very ripe or botrytized grapes are used. Because the last of such a harvest can occur well into November, the risks of rain (which dilutes the wine) and hail (which breaks the grapes or knocks them off the vines) are great. Vouvray, especially sweet Vouvray, ages so slowly that some of the best bottles aren't at their peak for 25 years or longer. Of course you don't have to wait that long, but Vouvray is a good enough value that it may be worthwhile buying a case and saving it for retirement or as part of your legacy.

Both the demi-sec and moelleux versions are good with mildly spicy dishes such as the Mulligatawny Soup on page 99 and the Braised Sea Scallops with Saffron, opposite. Goat cheese, plain or baked into a soufflé (see page 100), is magnificent. Vouvray in all levels of sweetness is delicious served alone as an aperitif. My favorite makers are Philippe Foreau of Domaine du Clos Naudin and Noël Pinguet of Domaine Huet.

COTEAUX DU LAYON

About 60 miles downstream from Vouvray is the small city of Angers. Another 5 to 10 miles downstream, inland from the southern banks of the Loire, is the Coteaux du Layon, a relatively large area that produces some of the sweetest (and some of the least expensive) Loire wines. Within the Coteaux du Layon are a number of villages, some of which have the right to include their name along with *Coteaux du Layon* on the bottle. French law, which

BRAISED SEA SCALLOPS WITH SAFFRON

Scallops have a delicate sweetness that makes them a perfect match for mildly sweet wines such as Vouvray demi-sec or even Vouvray moelleux. I also like to serve this dish with late-harvest riesling or gewurztraminer from Alsace or California. The saffron in this recipe goes beautifully with the scallops—saffron coupled with virtually any seafood is great—and gives a spicy note to the dish that draws out the complexity of the wine. A small amount of curry powder, cooked first in a little butter, can also be used instead of, or in combination with, the saffron.

Makes 4 main-course servings

1	**carrot,** chopped fine
3	**shallots,** chopped fine
3	**sprigs fresh thyme** (optional)
1	**imported bay leaf**
1/2	**cup dry** or **slightly sweet white wine**
1 1/2	**pounds large sea scallops**
1	**small bunch fresh chives,** chopped fine
1/2	**teaspoon saffron threads,** soaked for 20 minutes in a tablespoon of cold water
6	**tablespoons cold unsalted butter,** cut into 6 pieces **salt and pepper to taste**

Combine the carrot, shallots, thyme, and bay leaf with 2 cups of water in a small saucepan. Simmer gently until the vegetables soften, about 30 minutes, and pour in the wine. Simmer for 10 minutes more, and strain the liquid into a sauté pan just large enough to hold the scallops in a single layer. Discard the vegetables. Boil down the strained liquid to about half.

Pull off and discard the small muscle that runs up the side of each of the scallops. Cut the scallops crosswise into 1/4-inch-thick disks.

Five minutes before serving, put the scallops in the pan with the liquid. Put the pan over high heat and use a small ladle to baste the scallops while the liquid is coming to a simmer. When the scallops lose their sheen and turn opaque, after about 1 minute, transfer them to heated soup plates with a slotted spoon.

Over a low flame, whisk the chives, the saffron with its soaking water, and the butter into the poaching liquid while moving the pan quickly back and forth so the butter doesn't separate. Season the sauce to taste with salt and pepper and ladle it over the scallops. Provide soup or sauce spoons for your guests.

BLANC-MANGE

I was first introduced to blanc-mange when I cooked a
dinner in honor of the late Richard Olney, whose book
Yquem had just been published in English. Needless to
say, Château d'Yquem was served with the dessert—a
dessert that had to stay in the background but still lend
support to that wonderful wine. You can serve blanc-
mange with any Sauternes or other moderately sweet to
very sweet dessert wine.

Blanc-mange (sometimes blanc-manger) is a mildly
sweet yet richly flavored dessert made with almonds and
held together with gelatin. To succeed, there needs to be
just enough gelatin to get the almond "milk" to set—if
there's too much, your blanc-mange will be rubbery. The
dessert is supposed to be perfectly white, but I sacrifice
whiteness for flavor and toast the almonds. Blanc-mange
can also be made with other nuts such as hazelnuts or
pistachios.

Makes 8 servings

> 2 cups blanched almonds
> 1/2 teaspoon almond extract
> 2 1/2 teaspoons unflavored gelatin (a teaspoon less
>   than a whole packet), soaked for 15 minutes in
>   1/4 cup water
> 1/3 cup sugar
> 1 cup heavy cream
> 1/4 cup shelled, unsalted green pistachios (optional)

Preheat the oven to 350°F and toast the almonds on
a sheet pan for about 15 minutes, until they become
fragrant and turn a very pale brown.

Put the almonds in a blender with 2 cups warm
water—hold the lid on firmly—and purée for 2 minutes.
Strain the mixture through a fine-mesh strainer; push on
the mixture with a ladle to squeeze out as much liquid
as you can. Discard what doesn't go through the strainer.
Add the almond extract to the almond milk and stir in

the gelatin with its soaking liquid. If the almond milk has
cooled—in which case it won't dissolve the gelatin—
heat it gently in a saucepan until the gelatin dissolves.
Don't let it get too hot, which can cause it to separate.
Put the mixture in a bowl in the refrigerator—or over a
bowl of ice if you're in a hurry—until it feels cool to the
touch. This is important: if the mixture is too cold, the
gelatin will set prematurely; if it's too hot, it will take the
airiness out of the whipped cream when you add it.

Combine the sugar and heavy cream in a mixing
bowl and beat to medium peaks. Use a rubber spatula
to fold the whipped cream into the almond mixture.
Brush the inside of eight 5- or 6-ounce fez-shaped dari-
ole molds or 5- or 6-ounce ramekins with cold water—
this makes the blanc-mange easier to unmold—and
ladle in the blanc-mange mixture. Chill for at least an
hour in the refrigerator or until set.

Remove the inner peel from the pistachios by plunging
them in a pot of boiling water, boiling them for 1 minute,
draining in a strainer, and then rubbing them vigorously
in a kitchen towel. Chop the pistachios coarsely by pulsing them in a food processor or with a chef's knife.

When you're ready to serve, unmold the blanc-mange
on chilled plates by running a paring knife around the
inside of each ramekin, holding the plate on top, and
then inverting both the plate and mold. Sprinkle with the
chopped pistachios.

governs the amount of wine a maker can extract from a vineyard (the lower the yield, the better the wine), dictates lower yields for wines with the commune names attached to the words *Coteaux du Layon*. A few examples of communes are Beaulieu, St-Lambert, St-Aubin, Rochefort, and Chaume. To have *Chaume* on the label, the yields must be even lower than those for the other communes. Don't confuse Chaume with the rare and expensive Quarts de Chaume.

There are two wines, including the undeservedly obscure Bonnezeaux and the only somewhat better known and rare Quarts de Chaume, that are allowed to use their names without also including *Coteaux du Layon*. A bottle of wine labeled simply Coteaux du Layon can be had for very little since few people know what it is. When made well, a wine from the Coteaux du Layon shimmers like gold and captures the intense essence of chenin blanc—plump and delightfully acidic with deep yet subtle flavors of dried fruit, tropical fruit, honey, and flowers. A few of my favorite makers are Domaine de la Sansonnière, Domaine de Bablut, Domaine des Forges, Domaine des Petits Quarts, Château Pierre-Bise, Château de Suronde, Château Soucherie (Pierre-Yves Tijou), Domaine Ogereau, Jolivet, Château de la Guimonière, and Château des Rochettes. I serve wines from the Coteaux du Layon with mildly spicy dishes such as the Mulligatawny Soup on page 99; with goat cheeses or the Goat Cheese Soufflé on page 100, or alone as an aperitif.

BONNEZEAUX

Truly one of France's great wines and largely ignored, Bonnezeaux comes from vineyards around the small town of Bonnezeaux in the Coteaux du Layon. The wine is a golden aromatic nectar that captures the sweet and shimmering soul of chenin blanc. Its aroma reminds me of ripe fruit, dried apricots, and shellac, probably caused by aldehydes, alcohol-related compounds produced during fermentation. (Don't worry, some of the greatest sweet wines, including Château d'Yquem, have this characteristic shellac-like aroma.) Good examples of Bonnezeaux are beautifully balanced with layers of tropical fruits—some of them unrecognizable—interspersed with the honeylike and slightly bitter flavor of botrytis. Because of

Here is a bottle of Coteaux du Layon from the Domaine Ogereau, one of the region's most respected wine-makers. This wine is a step up from generic Coteaux du Layon because it has the name of the vineyard, Saint Lambert, on the label.

FRESH MORELS WITH CREAM

Here's a simple fricassée of creamed fresh morels. This dish goes with all sorts of off-dry to moderately sweet wines such as late-harvest rieslings from California, Alsace (vendange tardive), or Germany (Spätlese or Auslese).

Makes 4 first-course servings

1 pound fresh morels
4 tablespoons unsalted butter
¾ cup heavy cream
  salt and pepper to taste

If the morels are sandy or gritty, quickly submerge them in cold water, drain, and pat dry with paper towels. Heat the butter in a sauté pan over medium to high heat until it froths. Add the morels. Sauté the morels until they darken and become fragrant, about 5 minutes, tossing or stirring in the pan so they cook evenly.

Add the cream to the hot morels and simmer gently until the cream barely begins to thicken, about 2 minutes. Season to taste with salt and pepper and serve on hot plates.

Bonnezeaux's obscurity, many winemakers are unwilling to invest in the manpower needed to hand select grapes by making several trips to the vineyard. The result is that quality varies greatly. My favorite makers are René Renou and Château de Fesles. Unfortunately for bargain hunters, these are also the most expensive.

CHAUME

One of the villages in the Coteaux du Layon allowed to put its name on the bottle in addition to the words *Coteaux du Layon*, Chaume is best known because of Quarts de Chaume, an almost legendary wine made in a small area surrounding the village of Chaume. My favorite maker is Domaine Ogereau.

QUARTS DE CHAUME

In this small enclave is made an almost minuscule amount of luscious chenin blanc sweet wine. Quarts, which means "quarter," is a restricted area within Chaume that produces the best grapes. My two favorite makers are Domaine des Baumard and Château Pierre-Bise. On those special occasions when I treat myself to a bottle of Quarts de Chaume (it's expensive), I often encounter the aroma of toasted hazelnuts. Quarts de Chaume is much like Bonnezeaux (tasting them together is a lesson in the joy of chenin blanc), except richer and generally less acidic. With the possible exception of Château d'Yquem, Quarts de Chaume from a good maker rivals the greatest Sauternes.

SAVENNIÈRES

On the northern side of the Loire but to the southwest of Angers are grown some of the most renowned (but paradoxically now unknown) Loire white wines. Today most Savennières are made into long-aging dry wines, but in the 19th century and up to World War II, wines from Savennières were sweet. If you're lucky enough to find a bottle of sweet Savennières, marked moelleux, grab it. Hopefully, as sweet wines become more popular, more of these wines will again be made sweet. Sweet wines from Savennières contain very high levels of acid and can age for well over 20 years. My favorite maker is the Domaine du Closel, which has 100-year-old vines that have never been attacked by phylloxera.

MADERIZED WINES

When badly stored or stored too long, some white wines become maderized—the word comes from *Madeira*—meaning that they have begun to oxidize and their color has turned from pale yellow or green to amber.

Most of the time, especially when dry wines are involved, maderization is a fault (you're completely justified in sending a maderized wine back in a restaurant), but in some cases, such as sherry and certain vins de paille, maderization is encouraged by letting the wine come in contact with air and sometimes with heat.

Many vins de paille may remind you of mildly sweet sherry. I like to serve them with olives, before dinner, as I would a glass of sherry.

ALSACE

Alsatian sweet wines are among the greatest wines in the world, and because they are relatively undiscovered, while never cheap, they're still a bargain—a bottle costs about the same as a modest dinner for two. The aroma of Alsatian wines amazes me because it's more like that of a dry wine, with restrained fruit and sometimes even a mineral aroma, instead of the honey and caramel fragrances we associate with sweet wines. This fruit is balanced by a steely acidity that makes the first sip a magnificent surprise. Late-harvest Alsatian wines are also beautiful to look at, ranging from pale green to straw-colored to deep orange. The style of Alsatian wines depends a lot on the winemaker. Some, such as Zind-Humbrecht, make wines with lots of crisp acidity and concentrated yet restrained fruit. Others make wines that are softer, with less acid and a more pronounced fruitiness. The aroma and flavor of most Alsatian wines remind me of citrus fruits, especially grapefruit, with difficult-to-define undercurrents of papaya and pineapple.

Unlike German winegrowers, who almost always leave a little natural sugar in their wine by refrigerating it during fermentation to stop the yeasts, most Alsatian winegrowers allow their wine to ferment until there's no sugar left and the wine is bone-dry. Some wines, labeled *vendange tardive* (meaning late harvest), are harvested as late as November and are usually sweet (see When to Pick the Grapes, page 35). These wines must meet rigorous standards specifying the varietal (only four kinds of grape are permitted: riesling, muscat, gewurztraminer, and pinot gris), the minimum sugar concentration at harvest, and the quantity, which is very limited.

While vendange tardive wines are expensive, they're so intensely flavored and rich that a little bit goes a long way—I get as many as 15 servings out of a bottle. Even rarer and more expensive than vendange tardive wines are wines labeled *sélection de grains nobles*, made from individual botrytized grapes in the same way as a great Sauternes or German Trockenbeerenauslese. These wines are always sweet.

Every grape variety in Alsace produces a wine with a distinctive flavor and bouquet. Gewurztraminer is the easiest to recognize because it has a floral and spicy aroma that reminds me of dried tangerine peels. Riesling produces the most subtle and exciting sweet wines in Alsace. Pinot gris, sometimes called tokay, produces plumper, rounder wines with less acidity and a less pronounced varietal character than wine made from riesling.

Many of the best bottles of Alsatian wine specify the vineyard the wine comes from or that it comes exclusively from Grand Cru vineyards. A great deal of politics and controversy have entered into this Grand Cru

Here is an example of one of Alsace's rarest and most expensive wines, a sélection de grains nobles, made by harvesting individual wizened grapes. It is also from one of Alsace's greatest makers (Zind-Humbrecht) and from what many consider to be Alsace's finest vineyard, Clos Saint Urbain. The nose is redolent of candied fruit—in fact, it reminds me of a well-doused fruit cake—and the flavors of citrus and tropical fruit are concentrated and intense. The finish lasts forever.

MADELEINES

Because they're not very sweet, these scallop-shaped cakelike cookies make a lovely accompaniment to a sweet wine you're serving with dessert or with an afternoon snack. Proust had his epiphany munching on a madeleine while sipping a cup of tea, but I find a glass of crisp and aromatic Alsatian riesling or gewurztraminer far more inspiring.

To make madeleines, you need a special mold with scallop-shaped indentations, a nuisance to buy, but once it's in hand you can whip up madeleines in minutes. Look for a nonstick mold. This recipe is calculated for relatively large madeleines—3 inches long and 2 inches wide at the widest part.

Makes 24 madeleines

1 tablespoon softened butter (for the mold)
2 tablespoons flour (for the mold)
4 tablespoons unsalted butter
4 extra-large eggs, brought to warm room temperature in a bowl of hot tap water
4 tablespoons sugar
1/2 teaspoon grated lemon zest or vanilla extract
3/4 cup all-purpose flour

Preheat the oven to 425°F.

Brush or rub the inside of a madeleine mold with half the softened butter, refrigerate the mold for 10 minutes, and then rub or brush it with the remaining butter. Sprinkle the flour over each indentation and shake the mold back and forth so the flour evenly coats the indentations. Hit the back of the mold to get rid of excess flour. Refrigerate.

Heat the butter in a small saucepan over medium heat. After about 2 minutes you'll see specks of milk solids form on the bottom of the pan. When these milk solids turn pale brown and the butter has a butterscotch aroma, take the pan off the heat.

Combine the eggs, sugar, and lemon zest in the bowl of an electric mixer—you can also beat them by hand—and beat the mixture on high speed until it triples in volume and a ribbon about 1/2 inch thick falls from the beater when you lift it above the eggs, about 4 minutes.

Put the flour in a strainer and shake it over the eggs, folding it in as you go with a rubber spatula. Don't overwork the mixture but be careful to reach down to any flour that may have sunk to the bottom of the bowl. Pour the melted butter down the side of the bowl with the eggs—don't pour it straight over the eggs or they'll lose airiness. Use a rubber spatula to reach down and fold the melted butter and flour over and through the egg mixture. Fold for about 30 seconds. Don't worry if there's a little butter that isn't mixed into the eggs—better that than overworking the eggs.

Ladle the egg mixture into the mold, just filling each indentation with no excess coming higher than the rim of the mold. Bake until puffed and golden brown, about 10 minutes. Let cool for 5 minutes in the mold and then turn over to unmold the madeleines.

PINEAPPLES WITH KIRSCH AND RASPBERRIES

This is a great winter dessert, since pineapples are available year-round. It goes with virtually any sweet wine but especially with Sauternes or one of the lesser-known wines from the nearby villages of Cadillac, Cérons, Ste-Croix-du-Mont, or Loupiac.

Makes 6 servings

1   **medium pineapple,** leaves twisted off, skin cut off
2   **tablespoons good-quality kirsch**
     (Swiss brands are best)
1   **pint raspberries or other red berry** (optional)
one **10-ounce package frozen raspberries**
     (unsweetened), thawed (optional)

Cut the pineapple vertically into quarters. Cut off the strip of core that runs along the side of each of the quarters and slice the quarters about $1/3$ inch thick. Toss these wedges with the kirsch and the berries. If you're making a raspberry sauce, purée the thawed raspberries and work them through a fine-mesh strainer with the back of a small ladle. Serve on the side in a sauce boat.

system, however, such that some of Alsace's most famous vineyards have been left out. Many of these vineyards start with the name *Clos*, which is easiest remembered as an enclosure or patch. One of the most famous of these vineyards is Clos Saint Urbain, owned exclusively by the winemakers Zind-Humbrecht, where they make gewurztraminer, riesling, and pinot gris, sometimes labeled Tokay-Pinot Gris. The wine writer Robert Parker has called Clos Saint Urbain the "montrachet of Alsace." (Montrachet is deservedly France's most famous dry white wine.)

Other great vineyards include Clos Saint Imer, Clos Sainte Hune, Clos Gaensbroennel, Clos Saint Landelin, Clos Windsbuhl, Clos Zisser, and the tiny Clos Rebgarten. I don't recommend searching for a specific wine from these vineyards: instead, pick them out when you spot them. A few of my favorite makers are Lucien Albrecht, Paul Blanck, Albert Boxler, Marcel Deiss, Dopff, Hugel, Marc Kreydenweiss, Albert Mann, Charles Schleret, Pierre Sparr, Domaine Trimbach, and Zind-Humbrecht.

I don't serve Alsatian wines with dessert because their steely acidity doesn't work well with sweets. I serve them just before dinner, when everyone's taste buds are still in good shape, or with a first course. Unless your guests are very experienced wine drinkers, a glass of late-harvest Alsatian wine will amaze them. I serve Alsatian wines with, among other things, prosciutto and melon, Roast Figs (page 94; especially good with pinot gris), Madeleines (a great combo for the afternoon; see recipe on page 33), Hazelnut Biscotti (page 54), Mulligatawny Soup (page 99), Cheese Puffs (page 64), and Red or Pink Lentil Soup (page 123).

THE SOUTHWEST OF FRANCE

MONBAZILLAC

At first glance and sip, you might mistake a Monbazillac for a Sauternes, but to call Monbazillac the poor man's Sauternes is to do it an injustice. While it is true that a decent bottle of Monbazillac can be had for less than half the price of a modest Sauternes, Monbazillac has an identity all its own. Like Sauternes, Monbazillac is made with sauvignon blanc and sémillon, but it also contains a good amount of muscadelle grapes (see page 130). And again like Sauternes, Monbazillac is made by letting the grapes succumb to botrytis and making repeated trips to the vineyards to harvest only those grapes that are wizened with mold.

But while Monbazillac has a very similar structure to Sauternes—the levels of acidity and sweetness are about the same and the honeylike flavor

Even though winemaking laws in France are stricter than in a lot of places, conscientious winemakers often set higher standards for themselves than the law dictates. In Alsace grape juice destined for wines labeled vendange tardive, meaning late harvest, must have a potential alcohol of 13% for riesling and muscat and 14.3% for gewurztraminer and pinot gris. Because yeasts survive at these relatively low alcohol levels, vendange tardive wines aren't necessarily sweet. They are only sweet if the winemaker sets higher standards for him- or herself, picking the grapes when they have a higher concentration of sugar or stopping the fermentation before all the sugar has been fermented.

Wines labeled sélection de grains nobles have higher required potential alcohol levels (15.2% for riesling and muscat; 16.5% for gewurztraminer and pinot gris) and hence are always sweet.

On the other hand, it's also possible to encounter a sweet wine, usually from a Grand Cru vineyard, that isn't labeled vendange tardive or sélection de grains nobles, even though it has the legally required sugar levels. This is because the winemakers have set higher standards than those required by law.

of botrytis is evident—many Monbazillacs have a distinctive smoky aroma and flavor. Monbazillac is made in the Périgord, a region famous for its truffles and foie gras. Foie gras is a magnificent first course made even better when accompanied by a glass of chilled Monbazillac.

Although Monbazillac is classic with a slice of terrine of foie gras, I like to serve it with Chicken Liver Mousse (see recipe on opposite page) so I don't need a second mortgage. Monbazillac and other sweet wines from the southwest are also good served with the Crispy Apple Tart on page 70 or as an aperitif. My favorite Monbazillac makers are Christian Roche of the Domaine de l'Ancienne Cure (especially his Cuvée Abbaye) and Bruno Bilancini of Château Tirecul La Gravière (especially the expensive Cuvée Madame).

HAUT-MONTRAVEL

This is another wine that, having fallen from fashion, almost went extinct, but in the last couple of decades, a few dedicated winemakers are again making Haut-Montravel. Don't confuse it with Montravel, which is dry. There's so little Haut-Montravel around that it's hard to be picky about the maker. The only one I've been able to find is Château Puy-Servain Terrement, whose wine has an amazing aroma of a delicious red wine stew and a flavor of caramelized apples. I serve Haut-Montravel with a first course of foie gras (see photograph, right) or with a not-too-sweet dessert such as the Crispy Apple Tart on page 70.

SAUSSIGNAC

Less well known and usually less sweet than Monbazillac, Saussignac wines come from near a village about 8 miles west of Monbazillac, about 25 miles west of Bergerac, and 40 miles east of Bordeaux. Like Monbazillac, wines from Saussignac are made from sémillon, sauvignon blanc, and muscadelle. I find it difficult to tell the difference between Monbazillac and Saussignac, as both have the same characteristic smoky aroma and taste. Saussignacs vary a lot in quality and price. My favorite is Château Richard, from Richard Doughty (it tastes strikingly of saffron) and Domaine du Cantonnet. I serve Saussignac with simply prepared seafood such as whole baked fish.

FOIE GRAS

One good trick in a restaurant is to order a bottle of Sauternes, drink half of it with a slice of terrine of foie gras, and save the rest for dessert. Foie gras, especially terrine of foie gras served cold, makes the perfect foil for rich sweet wines.

For foie gras with the best flavor and texture, buy foie gras labeled *entier* or *bloc*, not *mousse*. Serve the foie gras cool in thick slices. Pass toasted bread at the table.

If you're serving hot foie gras as a first course or a main course, you'll need to buy the whole raw liver, thoroughly trim and clean it, cut it crosswise into $\frac{1}{2}$-inch-thick slices, and brown it quickly over high heat in a nonstick pan or iron skillet. Sweet wines such as Jurançon (moelleux or liquoreux), Monbazillac, and Sauternes; red sweet wines such as Banyuls; or even a glass of port all make great accompaniments to hot foie gras.

CHICKEN LIVER MOUSSE

While a little snack of foie gras always sounds like a good idea, it's not something you're likely to find at your local supermarket. Although chicken livers are a far cry from foie gras, this full-flavored mousse also works with sweet wines such as Monbazillac and Sauternes.

The concept behind this recipe is simple. Chicken livers are sautéed and puréed with butter; then the mixture is chilled and folded with whipped cream.

Makes 4 cups mousse (8 first-course servings or 15 hors d'oeuvres)

12 ounces (³/₄ pound) **chicken livers,** trimmed of any small threadlike blood vessels and fat
2 tablespoons pure olive oil
salt and pepper to taste
2 medium shallots, peeled, chopped fine
1 small clove garlic, peeled, chopped fine
¹/₂ teaspoon finely chopped fresh thyme or **marjoram** or **¹/₄ teaspoon dried thyme** or **marjoram**
¹/₄ cup port or **semi-dry Madeira** or **cream sherry**
2 tablespoons cognac (optional)
¹/₂ pound (2 sticks) **butter**
1 cup heavy cream, chilled

Rinse and drain the livers and pat them dry. In a sauté pan or skillet just large enough to hold the livers in a single layer, heat the olive oil over high heat until it begins to smoke. (It's essential that the pan be very hot or the livers will end up simmering in their own juices.) Season the livers with salt and pepper and lower them, one by one, into the hot skillet—stand back because chicken livers tend to spatter. Brown the livers for about 3 minutes on each side, until they feel firm to the touch. Use a slotted spoon to scoop them out of the pan and into a bowl.

Discard the cooked fat. Add the shallots, garlic, and herbs to the hot pan and stir them for about a minute, then pour in the port. Boil the port down to about half,

add the cognac, boil for about 15 seconds more, and pour the mixture over the livers. Let the livers cool for 10 minutes.

Cut the butter into six chunks and put these in the bowl with the livers. Let sit for about 15 minutes, allowing the livers to cool and the butter to soften slightly. (Don't, however, let the butter actually melt, since this will make the mixture heavy.) Purée the mixture in a food processor until smooth and then work it through a drum sieve or large strainer with the back of a large spoon or small ladle.

Beat the cream to medium peaks—not to stiff peaks or the mousse will be dry—and whisk a quarter of the cream into the liver mixture. Use a rubber spatula to fold the liver mixture with the rest of the cream, and season again to taste with salt and pepper. Cover the mousse with plastic wrap with the plastic pressed against the surface of the mousse (if allowed contact with air, the mousse will turn dark) and chill for 3 hours or overnight. Serve the mousse in individual 3-ounce ramekins or put it into a big bowl and pass it at the table. Chicken liver mousse is not stiff enough to slice.

SAUTÉED BONELESS PORK MEDALLIONS WITH PEACHES

Pork goes well with sweet wine, especially a Sauternes or Monbazillac. Depending on the time of year, other fruits such as pears and apples can be substituted for the peaches in this recipe. In the summer, I grill both peaches and pork alike.

Makes 6 main-course servings

one 2½- to 3-pound boneless pork loin
    salt and pepper to taste
 1 **tablespoon olive oil**, plus more for rubbing
 4 **ripe peaches**
 3 **tablespoons unsalted butter**
 1 **tablespoon sugar**

Trim any pieces of fat or membrane from the outside of the pork loin (or have the butcher do this for you).

Slice the pork loin into six plump, boneless medallions. Season them with salt and pepper and rub with olive oil. If you're not sautéing right away, the medallions can be refrigerated, covered, for up to 24 hours. Take them out of the refrigerator an hour before sautéing to let them come to room temperature.

An hour before sautéing, cut the peaches into eight wedges each, discarding the pits. If you're using pears or apples, peel and cut them at the last minute so they don't turn dark. Sauté the medallions in the olive oil for about 7 minutes on each side until they bounce back to the touch. Transfer the medallions to a warm place, pour off the cooked oil, and replace it with the butter. Put the peaches in the pan, sprinkle them with the sugar, and sauté them over medium heat until they turn golden brown, about 5 minutes on each side.

Put the medallions on hot plates and surround each portion with peach wedges.

PACHERENC DU VIC-BILH

Wines from Pacherenc du Vic-Bilh, located in the Béarn region (on the Atlantic side of the French Pyrenees), are made from petit manseng and the frightfully obscure arrufiat and courbu. Pacherenc du Vic-Bilh is sometimes compared unfavorably to Jurançon, but Pacherenc du Vic-Bilh from a good maker has very much its own identity, with an intense flavor of botrytis and good acidity. The flavor and aroma of Pacherenc du Vic-Bilh have been compared to rose petals, but to me the wines have a distinct aroma of carnations. My favorite makers are Domaine de l'Ancienne Cure (especially the Cuvée Abbaye), Château Tirecul La Gravière, Château Le Payral, Château Richard, Château Puy-Servain, and Château d'Aydie.

JURANÇON

Long one of my favorite little secrets, Jurançon is very much a wine of its own, in part no doubt because of the obscure grape variety, petit manseng, that it's made of. The wine from the village of Jurançon, near the city of Pau in the southwest, has been around a long time—at least since the middle ages, when both white and red wines were made. Today only white wines, both dry and sweet, are made around Jurançon. I've never tasted a dry Jurançon that was worth repeating, but the sweet versions are very special and often a great value. Jurançon sweet wine is made by letting the grapes dry on the vine before harvesting—a method called *passerillage*—rather than relying on botrytis to concentrate the grapes' sugar. Jurançon reminds me of peaches, cinnamon, mushrooms, and honey. Two of my favorite makers are Domaine Cauhapé, especially Cuvée Quintessence, and Domaine Bru-Baché.

LOOKING AT WINE

When comparing the color of two or more wines, put the glasses on a white surface such as a white tablecloth and look through the wine where it's farthest away from you in the glass. It's much easier to see the color of the wine this way than by holding the glass up to the light.

Above are a young vintage Maury, which is dark red or almost purple (left), and a 15-year-old Maury made in a rancio style that has a brick color reminiscent of tawny port. The vintage wine has an aroma of ripe currants, dates, and an undefinable floral smell that reminds me of a florist's shop. The flavor of fresh red berries dominates. The rancio-style Maury has a distinct aroma and flavor of coffee and toffee. Because both these wines have a lot of alcohol, they should be served cool—about 55°F.

Left: The butterscotch, honeylike flavors and mushroom aroma of this Jurançon La Quintessence from Domaine Bru-Baché is the perfect match for cured meats. Note that the wine is made from botrytrized grapes—essentially grapes that have been "cured."

THE LANGUEDOC-ROUSSILLON

The Languedoc is a huge region in southern France that runs along the Mediterranean from the Rhône River to Spain. (Provence is east of the Rhône Valley; the Languedoc, to the west.) For years Languedoc winemaking was limited to the production of the French equivalent to jug wine, the plastic liter bottle meant as an everyday beverage and little more. In the last 20 years, the quality of winemaking in the Languedoc has risen spectacularly, and vineyards that for years have lain fallow are now being planted with better grape varietals.

The sweet wines from four of Languedoc's villages were famous in the 19th century and, at least until recently, virtually unknown outside of the region. All the wine from these villages is made from muscat grapes, usually muscat blanc à petits grains.

The small town of Frontignan has for centuries produced a wine—Muscat de Frontignan—from muscat blanc à petits grains. Like so many sweet wines, it was popular in the 17th, 18th, and 19th centuries but lost its glamour in the 20th. Frontignan, similar to but even sweeter and more intensely fruity than Muscat de Beaumes-de-Venise is a good value since so few people know about it. Lunel, even less known than Frontignan, is again starting to produce muscat wines, similar to Muscat de Beaumes-de-Venise, but somewhat more intense and often less expensive. Mireval, near Frontignan and producing virtually identical wine, has its own appellation contrôlée, allowing it to distinguish itself on the label. Muscat de Saint-Jean-de-Minervois comes from a region in the Languedoc close to Spain; it is made much like Muscat de Beaumes-de-Venise but is less known and usually a better value.

Roussillon, right across the Pyrenees mountains from the Catalonia region of Spain, borders the Mediterranean Sea to the east and the Languedoc to the north and west. The region's hot climate tempered by relatively mild breezes makes it perfect for growing grapes for intense rich wines, especially sweet wines.

RIVESALTES

More muscat wine is made in Rivesaltes, an ancient village along the Agly River in the Roussillon, than in any other place in the world. Strangely, Rivesaltes wine is little known outside of France. There are two main kinds of Rivesaltes, Muscat de Rivesaltes and "plain" Rivesaltes, both made by adding alcohol to the fermenting wine. Muscat de Rivesaltes can be made with both muscat blanc à petits grains or the higher-yielding muscat of Alexandria. Muscat de Rivesaltes is fresh and fruity—it should be drunk

---

VIN DE PAILLE

The grapes for vin de paille—*paille* is French for "straw"—are dried on mats, traditionally made from straw, before being turned into wine. Vins de paille were popular in years past, when people had more of a taste for sweet wine and before spirits were widely used to make fortified wines. Today many of the wines that were once vins de paille are now made as fortified wines. Fortunately a few ambitious winemakers are experimenting once again with vins de paille.

In the Jura, in eastern France, grapes are hung to dry into raisins instead of being spread out on the traditional straw mats. L'Etoile, a small appellation in the Jura, is sometimes exported as *vin jaune*—a dry wine allowed to oxidize much like sherry—and at other times as sweet vin de paille made from the obscure savagnin grape.

A very limited amount of vin de paille is made in Hermitage, an area in the Rhône Valley best known for its great red wines. It takes 100 pounds of grapes to make 2 gallons of vin de paille, so needless to say, it is expensive.

Wine called *passerillé* in French is similar to vin de paille, but instead of the grapes being dried off the vine, they are allowed to dry while still on the vine. In Italy vins de paille and wines made from grapes that have been allowed to dry on the vine are both called *passito*.

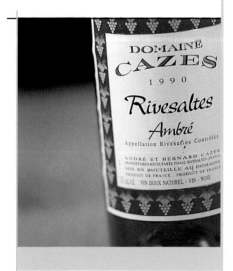

Rivesaltes ambré is one of Rivesaltes's most interesting wines because it can be made with an array of grape varieties, including white grenache and obscure strains found only in France's southwest. It's a delightful drink that almost reminds me of tawny port, except that it's lighter and pleasantly pink. Rivesaltes ambré should be served chilled and is even good over ice with a twist of lemon.

within the year—and makes a light and lovely aperitif. Because most wines don't actually taste like grapes, the first sip of Rivesaltes makes an immediate impression. Once your nose gets used to muscat's grapey aroma, other fragrances such as citrus, roasted nuts, and exotic flowers begin to emerge.

Wine labeled simply as Rivesaltes can be red, white, or amber (ambré) and can be made from a number of grapes, including red or white grenache, malvoisie (malvasia), and the two muscat grapes—muscat of Alexandria and muscat blanc à petit grains—allowed for Muscat de Rivesaltes. Unlike Muscat de Rivesaltes, regular Rivesaltes cannot be sold until it has aged at least 16 months The style of the wine depends on the maker; some prefer a rancio style, achieved by leaving the casks out in the sun, while some use a solera system (see The Solera System, page 81) to ensure a consistent style. Rivesaltes ambré is allowed contact with air and heat, which is how it gets its characteristic color and butterscotch/oxidized flavor. Rivesaltes ambré that's aged for five years or more is labeled hors d'âge. Rivesaltes ambré, like Muscat de Rivesaltes, makes a lovely aperitif when lightly chilled.

BANYULS

The French have always been fond of aperitifs based on wine, such as vermouth, made by infusing wine with herbs and/or letting the wine age in barrels in the sun. Banyuls is a port-like wine that, horror of horrors, happens to be delicious over ice with a twist of lemon. Admittedly I'd be more reverent about a fine old Banyuls Grand Cru, saving it for after dinner or at least skipping the ice and lemon, but you get the idea.

Banyuls, like Rivesaltes, is made in Roussillon, so close to the border it's practically in Spain. Some of its ancient terraced vineyards are in and around Collioure, a village made famous by Matisse and Dérain. Banyuls is made from both red grenache and a very dark variety called grenache noir. Once the grapes have been pressed and alcohol added to stop fermentation, the partially fermented wine is kept in contact with the grape skins to give the wine its characteristic deep color.

Banyuls is made in two styles. The first is a relatively fresh vintage-dated style that's bottled without exposure to heat or air, much like vintage port. More expensive vintage Banyuls, called Banyuls Grand Cru, must be aged in casks for a minimum of 30 months. There is also an oxidized or rancio style made by aging in small barrels or glass demi-muids (which look vaguely like Alhambra bottles) that are allowed to sit out in the sun. Some makers use a solera system by adding and removing wine while never fully emptying the barrels (see The Solera System, page 81).

OXTAILS BRAISED IN BANYULS

When simmered for hours in wine, oxtails are one of the most sublime of braised things, and unlike many stew meats, they never dry out. I got the idea of using Banyuls from a recipe for lamb in an old favorite book, *La Bonne Cuisine du Périgord*—in which they suggest using Monbazillac—and the memory of a delicious oxtail dish made with grapes. When buying your oxtail pieces, look for the biggest ones you can find—they look more dramatic on the plate. This recipe can be made ahead because it's even better the next day. Most traditional stews are thickened with flour, but I leave the sauce as it is, a concentrated broth, and serve it and the vegetables around the oxtails on heated soup plates.

Makes 6 main-course servings

- 12 large, thick oxtail rounds (8 ounces each)
  salt and pepper to taste
- 6 tablespoons olive oil, vegetable oil, or bacon fat
- 3 tablespoons butter
- 2 medium carrots, peeled and sliced
- 3 medium onions, chopped
- 4 cloves garlic, peeled and crushed
- one 750 cl bottle Banyuls, Ste-Croix-du-Mont, Cérons, less expensive Sauternes, or muscat such as Muscat de Rivesaltes
- 6 medium tomatoes, peeled, seeded, and chopped
- 7 sprigs fresh thyme or 1/2 teaspoon dried
- 1 small bunch parsley
- 2 imported bay leaves
- 1 pound whole wild mushrooms such as chanterelles or morels, or cultivated mushrooms, cut in quarters (optional)
- 2 tablespoons butter, or more as needed (optional; for sautéing the mushrooms)
  good-quality wine vinegar to taste

Season the oxtails liberally with salt and pepper. Preheat the oven to 350°F.

Heat the oil in a wide, heavy-bottomed pot large enough to hold the oxtails. (If you don't have a large enough pot, brown the oxtails in something else and layer them, once browned, in the pot.) Brown the oxtails on both sides over high heat. Reserve on a platter; pour the cooked fat out of the pot and discard. Let the pot cool slightly then add the butter, carrots, onions, and garlic and cook over medium heat, stirring with a wooden spoon, until the onions turn translucent, about 20 minutes.

Nestle the oxtails in the pot with the vegetables, pour over the wine, and add the tomatoes. Bring to a gentle simmer on top of the stove. Make a bouquet garni by tying up the thyme, parsley, and bay leaves with a piece of string. If you're using dried thyme, wrap the herbs in a piece of cheesecloth. Nestle the bouquet garni in with the oxtails.

Cover the top of the pot with a sheet of aluminum foil and put on the lid. Slide the pot in the oven and let stew for 5 hours. Check periodically to make sure the liquid isn't boiling—a bubble should come up about every 2 seconds—and adjust the heat accordingly.

Gently transfer the oxtails to a bowl using a skimmer or slotted spoon. Bring the liquid with the vegetables to a gentle simmer with the pot slightly off center in relation to the burner—this causes the fat floating on top to move to one side. Use a small ladle to skim off fat that floats to the top. Continue simmering and skimming the stewing liquid for about 20 minutes. If you're serving the oxtails the next day, just put the liquid in the refrigerator and when the fat congeals take it off with a spoon.

About 20 minutes before you're ready to serve, reheat the oxtails in their degreased braising liquid. If you're using the mushrooms, sauté them in butter for 5 to 10 minutes—make sure any liquid they release evaporates—and season with salt and pepper. Season the sauce as needed with salt and pepper and a tablespoon or two of vinegar. Serve the oxtails surrounded with sauce and topped with the optional mushrooms.

Among the best Banyuls are Alain Soufflet and Laurent Escapac's Domaine de la Casa Blanca (photograph above), wines from the Domaine de Jau, and wines from the Domaine du Mas Blanc.

MAURY

It's sometimes hard to tell the difference between a Banyuls and a wine made in the nearby region of Maury. There are those who claim that Maury wines have a distinct scent of black currants, but so does Banyuls. I'm more reminded of cocoa. Like Banyuls, Maury is made in two styles: a rancio style, priced according to how many years it has spent in cask or in glass containers called *demi-muids* out in the sun; and a vintage style that isn't allowed to oxidize. Vintage Maury, like vintage port, should be drunk at one sitting—I serve it with cheese—while the rancio style can be kept open in the bottle for months. The makers even use a regular wine cork for the vintage and a twist-off reusable cork for the rancio style. Maury wines are harder to find than Banyuls and are almost exclusively from Mas Amiel, a reputable maker that produces, in addition to a vintage wine, a 10-year-old called Cuvée Spéciale and a 15-year-old called Prestige.

Virtually all sweet red wines benefit from being poured into a decanter to breathe, if only for a few minutes. Some red wines, especially young wines, may not have thrown any sediment and can simply be poured into the decanter; for information about decanting older wines, see page 12.

How far ahead to decant depends on the age of the wine: a wine that's young can benefit from having a couple of hours to breathe; an old wine should be served within minutes of being decanted. My favorite decanter has a thin neck and a squat bottom that exposes the wine to a maximum amount of air.

THE RHÔNE VALLEY

The Rhône Valley used to be known for its vins de paille, but the labor-intensive tradition has all but died out. A few innovative winemakers are doing their best to revive the tradition and have come up with some (frightfully expensive) examples. Late-harvest Condrieu is still available but hard to find. In the southern Rhône, winemakers are making fortified wines by adding alcohol to fermenting grenache grapes.

RASTEAU

Rasteau is a town in the southern part of the Rhône Valley better known for its often excellent dry Côtes du Rhône than for its sweet fortified wine. Like dry Rasteau, sweet Rasteau is made with red grenache grapes. Well-made late-harvest Rasteau tastes a lot like Banyuls, late-harvest zinfandel, or even port. It's one of my favorite wines to serve with cheese.

CAIRANNE

Like Rasteau, Cairanne is a village in the southern Rhône Valley that makes a sweet, fortified version of its well-respected Côtes de Rhone.

MUSCAT DE BEAUMES-DE-VENISE

For those who claim not to like sweet wines, Muscat de Beaumes-de-Venise, which bursts with the aroma of fresh apricots, is an immediate sell. Beaumes-de-Venise is a sleepy little village in the southern Rhône Valley not far from Rasteau. Made from the best kind of muscat grapes—muscat blanc à petits grains—this wine becomes fortified when alcohol is added to the fermenting must to stop the yeasts. The resulting Muscat de Beaumes-de-Venise is a fortified wine, but one without the richness and heaviness sometimes associated with port and other port-like red fortified wines.

CLAIRETTE DE DIE

Clairette is a grape that is used to produced a lightly sparkling, refreshing, fruity drink, Clairette de Die, named after the town of Die along the banks of the Drôme River, east of the Rhône Valley. Because Clairette de Die contains very little alcohol—usually about 7%—it makes a refreshing and light summer drink. The best versions of Clairette de Die, specifically Tradition, are made with a blend of clairette and muscat à petits grains.

The label on this late-harvest wine from Condrieu says: *"Vendangé par tries de pourriture noble et de grains passerillés." Vendangé* means harvested; a *trie* is a trip out to the vineyard to select and handpick the grapes. Many *tries* are essential to making some sweet wines because grapes reach the optimum degree of overripeness at different times.

Pourriture noble is botrytis and *grains passerillés* are grapes that have dried and become like raisins on the vine. Hence this phrase—roughly translated as "harvested by repeated selections of grapes with noble rot and grapes dried on the vine"—underlines the fact that this wine combines two different techniques for getting extra sugar out of a grape.

CONDRIEU

The village of Condrieu is best known for its dry wines made from the viognier grape—wines with a distinct aroma so spicy and floral that you think the wine is going to be sweet, until you taste it. Until the last decade, Condrieu was virtually the only place that viognier was grown. The grape has since caught on in other places but still shows itself at its best in this village. A small amount of late-harvest viognier is also made in Condrieu. Because of their rarity, wines from Condrieu are expensive. Late-harvest versions are very rare indeed and correspondingly pricy.

CHAMPAGNE

In its natural state, the wine used to make French Champagne is extremely dry and contains a large proportion of acid. Most Champagne is very lightly sweetened by adding a sweet syrup, called *dosage*, the formula for which is usually secret. The amount of dosage added determines the sweetness of the wine. Champagne labeled brut or nature contains little if any dosage; extra dry contains a bit more; and demi-sec enough to make the wine distinctly sweet. I serve Champagne demi-sec after dessert and coffee—a refreshing surprise and one that keeps the party going. The Champagne Nectar Impérial from Moët & Chandon is only mildly sweet and has a lovely chalky nose.

Italy

Unlike France, which for the most part has clearly delineated winemaking regions, Italy is a patchwork of vineyards planted in often obscure grape varieties. The combination of ancient traditions and idiosyncratic winemaking styles makes Italy's sweet wines endlessly fascinating. Many of Italy's best sweet wines are *passito*—the Italian equivalent of France's vin de paille or passerillé—made by letting the grapes turn into raisins, either on the vine, on racks inside, or spread out on straw mats to dry in the sun. A few fortified wines—the most famous is Marsala—are also made this way. Compared to France and other places, wines made from botrytized grapes are relatively unusual in Italy.

THE NORTHEAST

Trentino–Alto Adige, the Veneto, and Friuli–Venezia Giulia make up Italy's northeast. All of these regions have for centuries been influenced by Venice and by such a mix of climates, grapes, and peoples that it's hard to assign them a unifying identity, except that they all produce a wide variety of delicious sweet wines.

In Alto Adige, at the very top of northern Italy, some amazingly aromatic sweet wines are made. The best-known sweet wines are made from one of two varieties of moscato—moscato giallo (goldenmuskateller) and moscato rosa (rosenmuskateller)—as well as botrytized chardonnay, sauvignon blanc, and pinot blanc. Unfortunately these wines are so hard to find that choosing a favorite maker may not be an option. Franz Haas and Josef Niedermayr are two of the best known.

In Trentino a kind of vin santo—spelled *vino santo*—is made from the obscure nosiola grape, which is rich and vibrant with acidity. The estate of Pojer & Sandri produce a wine called Essenzia (no relation to the Hungarian variety) that has a citrus aroma and a lovely clean crispness on the palate.

Opposite: Here I present a French wine, a Cadillac from a village near Sauternes (right), and an Italian Recioto di Soave from Gini. The Cadillac is redolent of citrus—especially grapefruit—and butterscotch, while the recioto has a mineral perfume and a distinct pine-like flavor, perhaps from new wood. Both are similarly sweet.

Below: Confini is a luscious late-harvest pinot grigio from Italy's Friuli region. It is made by Alvaro Pecorari of Lis Neris, who was inspired to make this sweet wine by Zind-Humbrecht in Alsace.

The Veneto, east and south of Trentino–Alto Adige and home to Venice, produces massive quantities of well-known dry Soave and Valpolicella and minute quantities of rare and delicious Recioto di Soave, a white wine, and Recioto della Valpolicella, a red. A Recioto di Gambellara is also made from garganega grapes, the same grapes used to make dry Soave. My favorite, La Biancara, has rich flavors of exotic fruits, a little wood, and lots of sprightly acidity. Vin santo, unusual to find outside of central Italy, is also produced in small amounts. Wines from Breganze, little known until recently, were made famous by Fausto Maculan, who produces the rare and expensive Torcolato and the even rarer and pricier Acininobili.

Finally from Friuli–Venezia Giulia, near Italy's border with Slovenia, comes picolit, rare and expensive, and the less rare but equally delicious Verduzzo di Cialla and Verduzzo di Ramandolo.

RECIOTO DI SOAVE

For anyone who remembers the indifferent jugs of dry white wine from the Veneto sold as Soave, a well-made Soave Classico and especially a sweet Recioto di Soave make delightful surprises. Recioto di Soave is rare and expensive and captures the essence of ripe garganega grapes, an aroma that reminds me of overripe bananas. Most Recioto di Soave is made from grapes that have been dried off the vine—sometimes for almost six months—but some winemakers have been experimenting with botrytized versions. Some of the best makers of Recioto di Soave are Roberto Anselmi, Claudio and Sandro Gini, and Leonildo Pieropan.

RECIOTO DELLA VALPOLICELLA

Many of us are familiar with the red wine Amarone, made by drying the grapes normally used to make Valpolicella. Drying the grapes concentrates the sugar, giving the winemaker the choice of making a dry wine with a lot of alcohol (such as Amarone) or a sweet wine in which the fermentation is stopped before all the sugar is fermented (such as Recioto della Valpolicella). The fermentation is stopped with alcohol, making Recioto della Valpolicella not only a sweet wine but a fortified one as well. Perhaps because these wines are so alcoholic and fruity—they smell of ripe berries—they often remind me of California wines. A few of the better-known makers are Allegrini (my favorite), Bussola, Masi, and Quintarelli. These wines are delicious with cheese, including the Goat Cheese Soufflés on page 100, and with the Bacon and Gruyère Tart on page 89. Don't try pairing them with desserts.

RECIOTI

I'm forever amazed that every single dessert wine is different. In northeastern Italy, they make an equivalent to the French vin de paille and Tuscan vin santo called recioto by letting specially selected, very ripe grapes partially dry out, which concentrates their sugar, before they are fermented. About a third of the grape juice evaporates during the drying, so needless to say, recioti are expensive.

Red Recioto della Valpolicella is probably the best known, but Recioto di Soave, which is white, is not at all reminiscent of dry Soave and has a flavor that reminds me distinctly of tropical fruits.

Two relatively well-known recioti are Acininobili and Torcolato (shown above), both made in Breganze, but there are also recioti made from chardonnay, muscat, and sauvignon blanc. Other recioti include d'Arancio from the Colli Euganei, a recioto from garganega grapes, and, most unusual, a late-harvest chardonnay called Colori d'Autunno.

BREGANZE

Breganze is a relatively obscure region in northeastern Italy. Two of Breganze's most famous sweet wines (recioto), made by the innovative Fausto Maculan, are Torcolato and the rare Acininobili. Both are made from vespaiola and tocai (not to be confused with tokay) grapes. Torcolato has a particular aroma and character unlike any other wine. As it warms in the glass, it reminds me of bananas cooked with rum and sprinkled with raisins. On the palate it's rich and buttery. Acininobili is a beautiful golden nectar much like Torcolato but with flavors that are even more intense. Its aroma reminds me of orange pekoe tea sweetened with honey.

RECIOTO DI GAMBELLARA

Made in the Veneto, near Soave, Gambellara is for the most part an indifferent wine, like most Soave. Recently, however, I encountered an expensive and delicious recioto version, La Biancara, that smells of dates and frothy cooked butter and tastes the way old books smell.

CONFINI

This is a single wine made by a single maker in Italy's Friuli region, but it is such an odd and tasty treat that it deserves its own mention. According to Kermit Lynch, who imports Confini, the winemaker—Alvaro Pecorari of Lis Neris—is such a dedicated fan of Zind-Humbrecht in Alsace that he decided to make his own late-harvest pinot grigio. It seems he has succeeded. You'd never guess this wine was sweet by smelling it. It has an almost steely, mineral aroma and a citrus flavor that, in fact, remind me of Alsatian wines. On the palate it is soft and luscious with rich flavors like peaches and cream but with plenty of acid so it doesn't get monotonous or seem too sweet. It's amazing when tasting Confini to imagine the leap from the light and crisp wines we associate with pinot grigio to this wine, so rich, so redolent of fruit, and so reminiscent of the way wine

is made in France. This is a great food wine that I especially like with roast pork, chicken, or seafood cooked with cream.

PICOLIT

This rare wine from Friuli is named after the grapes—picolit—from which it is made. Picolit are difficult grapes to grow, making the wine expensive. Picolit was appreciated in the 18th century when it was compared to Tokaji from Hungary, something hard to imagine today, since picolit is much less intensely aromatic and flavorful. Nowadays picolit is having a small renaissance due to the efforts of a couple of dedicated winemakers. Its best known makers are Abbazia di Rosazzo, Dorigo, Giovanni Dri, Ronchi di Cialla, Ronchi di Manzano, and La Viarte.

VERDUZZO FRIULANO

A similar but less prestigious (and to me more interesting) sweet wine than picolit, verduzzo friulano is made by some of the same makers from the easier-to-grow verduzzo grape. The few examples of verduzzo that I've tried smell and taste distinctly of licorice. The best verduzzo friulano comes from Ramandolo, a subregion of Friuli, and the best makers are Dario Coos, Giovanni Dri, Ronchi di Cialla, Ronchi di Manzano (see photograph, at left), and Roberto Picech. Walter Filiputti makes a beautiful orange, not-too-sweet Verduzzo Friulano with a citrus aroma and a flavor that reminds me distinctly of green apples.

PROSCIUTTO WITH FIGS

The fact is, I could eat prosciutto with anything (or nothing) almost every day of the year. When summer arrives, out comes the prosciutto and anything I can think of to serve with it. Melon is the most obvious but a little sweet for most wines; papaya and mangos are both great, but figs are best.

Because the combination of prosciutto and figs is both savory and only mildly sweet, you can serve most sweet wines without the wines being obliterated by strong flavors. Avoid, however, red sweet wines, because their tannins taste odd with the figs. A late-harvest (vendange tardive) Alsatian riesling or pinot gris (sometimes called tokay) is magnificent, as is a German Auslese.

Makes 6 first-course servings

1 pound thinly sliced (but not paper-thin) **prosciutto such as Prosciutto di Parma, San Daniele,** or **Serrano ham**
24 ripe figs

I like to give each guest a plate and then pass a basket of figs and a plate of prosciutto so people can help themselves, but if you want to be more formal, fan the figs out by cutting them vertically in two directions and unfolding each quarter. Drape the slices of prosciutto over each serving.

CENTRAL ITALY

By central Italy, I mean primarily Tuscany and Umbria. Other than Chianti, Tuscany is of course best known for vin santo, but there are also Tuscan sweet wines made from the aleatico grape, which smells a little bit like muscat. For the most part, aleatico is a red grape—there is a rare bianco version—that's used to make sweet wines in a variety of places, including Elba and Corsica. They also make vin santo in Umbria, as well as an off-dry and sometimes botrytized Orvieto. Near Rome, in Lazio (Latium), at least one producer makes a sweet aleatico wine.

VIN SANTO

Italy's best-known sweet wine, vin santo, comes in so many styles and flavors that virtually every bottle is different. Much of this is because vin santo is made by small makers who don't bother making the wine on a commercial scale but like to have it on hand to offer as a traditional gesture of hospitality. While there are laws governing how vin santo is made, every maker makes vin santo somewhat differently.

Most vin santo is made in Tuscany, where it has long been served as dessert with little cookies called biscotti (see recipe, page 54). Vin santo is traditionally made from dried malvasia and trebbiano (the lesser quality of the two), but recent laws also allow more familiar varietals such as sauvignon blanc, pinot gris, and chardonnay.

Vin santo gets much of its character from having been sealed up and aged in wooden casks for at least three years and often as long as ten. The casks are filled only three-quarters full and are left in a warm place, at times out in the sun, causing the wine to take on an oxidized flavor. A few of my favorite makers are Avignonesi, Capezzana, Isole e Olena, Sant'Anna, and Selvapiana.

FRASCATI

A small town just outside of Rome, Frascati is better known for its dry (and rather ordinary) white wines than for its sweet wine, Cannellino, made from malvasia and trebbiano. The only Cannellino I've been able to track down is made by Cantine Conte Zandotti (see photograph, above). It tastes strikingly of strawberries and makes a lovely aperitif. It's too light to be served later in the meal and should definitely not be served with dessert.

MOSCADELLO DI MONTALCINO

It's hard to imagine that this light and refreshing moscato, made from the rare moscadelletto strain of muscat grapes, is made in the same place as the intense red Brunello di Montalcino. Moscadello di Montalcino is hard to find, so when you see it, pick it up.

PASSITO DI SAGRANTINO DI MONTEFALCO

Sagrantino is a red grape grown in Umbria's Montefalco region. More and more Sagrantino is being made into dry wines, but it is traditionally used to make sweet wines from partially dried-out grapes. I recommend Passito di Sagrantino from Arnaldo-Caprai, which has a distinct aroma and flavor of wild cherries—more specifically, wild cherry Life Savers—and a structure a little bit like a ruby port. It also has the flavor of wood, which is not at all unpleasant.

THE NORTHWEST

Italy's northwest can be divided into four regions—Piemonte (Piedmont), Valle d'Aosta, Liguria, and Lombardia (Lombardy). All of these regions are better known for their dry wines than for their sweet wines, which tend to be quite rare. Some, including a passito made from pinot grigio, from grapes grown near the village of Nus, I've only read about and have never tasted. Near the village of Chambave they make a sweet moscato, which again, I've never tasted.

Piedmont is famous for its great red wines, Barolo and Barbaresco, both made from the nebbiolo grape, but it may be even better known as the source of Asti Spumante, the sparkling cousin of the far more delicious Moscato d'Asti. Sweet wines include Brachetto—a sparkling red wine—and Passito di Caluso, made from the erbaluce grape.

In Liguria, a stretch of coastline that forms the Italian Riviera, are found the famed villages of Cinque Terre, which aren't accessible by car and where the sweet wine Sciacchetrà is made. It comes in three varieties: *naturale*, *amabile*, and *liquoroso*, in ascending order of sweetness.

Lombardy's vineyards make use of a confusing plethora of grape varieties. The only sweet wine I know of is Moscato di Scanzo, made near Bergamo. In his *Wine Atlas of Italy* (1990), Burton Anderson describes it as "[having] a warm mahogany colour and aromas that bring to mind spices, exotic fruits, and burnished wood."

BRACHETTO D'ACQUI

Brachetto is a red grape used in Piedmont to make a sparkling red wine, Brachetto d'Acqui. Much of Brachetto d'Acqui is indifferent, but a bottle from a good maker makes a lovely aperitif—or an inexpensive alternative to champagne at brunch. It reminds me a little of sweet Beaujolais with bubbles. Look for wines made by Banfi, Ivaldi, and Pian dei Sogni.

MOSCATO D'ASTI

For anyone who has tasted Asti Spumante, Moscato d'Asti, made nearby with the same grapes, is a beautiful surprise. Never complicated or sophisticated, but lightly sparkling, intensely fruity, and with only about 5% alcohol, it's a little reminiscent of hard cider but more beguiling. No doubt in part because laws governing the production of Moscato d'Asti are stricter than those for Asti Spumante, Moscato d'Asti has a cleaner and more intensely fruity flavor. It makes a refreshing and lively summer drink that's eminently quaffable. I serve it as an aperitif or even with breakfast or at a picnic. Moscato d'Asti is too light to serve as a dessert wine. Dozens of makers produce Moscato d'Asti, and I've yet to taste one I haven't liked. Pictured below is one from a top producer, De Forville.

PASSITO DI CALUSO

One of the few sweet wines from Piedmont, Passito di Caluso is made from the erbaluce grape. Erbaluce is also used to make dry wines, but it shows itself at its best when used to make passito with a distinct flavor of raisins. Very little Passito di Caluso is exported. The only two makers I've encountered in the United States are Luigi Ferrando, who calls his passito Solativo, and Orsolani.

HAZELNUT BISCOTTI

In Tuscany these crunchy little cookies are traditionally served with vin santo. They differ from most other cookies because they are baked twice, and in this version because they contain both ground and whole hazelnuts. In addition to hazelnuts, these cookies are flavored with cinnamon. A good trick with cinnamon: buy a small jar of cinnamon sticks, grind them in a blender, and work the cinnamon through a fine-mesh strainer—the cinnamon will be much more aromatic.

Makes about 25 biscotti

2$\frac{1}{2}$ cups hazelnuts (about 1 pound)
2$\frac{1}{4}$ cups flour (plus more for rolling out dough
    and for baking sheet)
 $\frac{2}{3}$ cup sugar
 1 tablespoon ground cinnamon, preferably
    fresh-ground (see above)
 1 teaspoon ground cloves
 2 teaspoons vanilla extract
 1 packet (2$\frac{1}{2}$ teaspoons) active dry yeast, softened in
    3 tablespoons warm (not hot) water and combined
    with 1 tablespoon flour
 4 eggs
  butter (for baking sheet)

Preheat the oven to 350°F.

Spread the nuts on a baking sheet and bake until pale brown and fragrant, about 15 minutes. Rub them together while still hot in a kitchen towel to remove their papery skins. Don't worry if the skins don't all come off.

Combine 1 cup hazelnuts with the flour, sugar, cinnamon, and cloves in a food processor and process for about 2 minutes. Add the vanilla, the yeast mixture, and the eggs and process for about 30 seconds more. Dump the dough out onto a work surface and thoroughly knead in the rest of the hazelnuts so they're evenly distributed in the dough. Rub a baking sheet with butter. Sprinkle the dough with flour and shape it into a rectangle about

4 inches wide, an inch thick, and 16 inches long. Place the rectangle on the baking sheet, cover with a moist towel or a sheet of plastic wrap, and let sit in a warm place for 2 hours.

Preheat the oven to 350°F and bake the loaf for about 30 minutes until well browned. Transfer to a work surface with a spatula and let cool for 10 minutes. Cut the flattened loaf crosswise and diagonally into about 25 strips, each about $\frac{1}{2}$ inch thick.

Arrange the biscotti on the baking sheet again and bake for 15 minutes. Turn over and bake for 10 minutes more. Biscotti will last up to 2 weeks in a tightly sealed plastic bag or for months in the freezer.

Leftmost is Luigi Ferrando's Solativo, a Passito di Caluso that has a delicate floral fragrance with notes of vanilla and butterscotch and on the palate the taste of honeysuckle; in the middle is Passito di Caluso from Orsolani, which is the sweetest (notice it's also the darkest) of the three; and to the right is another Passito di Caluso from Ferrando, but this one is from 1994, before he started calling his wine Solativo. It has an aroma that reminds me distinctly (and pleasantly) of cheese rinds and has a delicate pine flavor, probably from new wood but not from oak.

THE EAST

By eastern Italy, I mean the long strip that runs along the Adriatic coast south of Venice and includes the regions of Emilia-Romagna, the Marches, and the Abruzzi. Emilia-Romagna's best-known sweet wine is made from lambrusco grapes, but for the most part the quality is low. More interesting are wines made from the albana grape, an ancient variety sometimes called Greco or Greco di Ancona. Malvasia is also used to make both amabile and passito styles. Down the coast, in the Marches, the verdicchio grape is used to produce both dry and sweet white wines. I've yet to encounter a sweet wine from the Abruzzi.

ALBANA DI ROMAGNA

While Emilia-Romagna is the region where the well known lambrusco is made (see below), I prefer wines made from the albana grape, which apparently has been around since Roman times. Albana wines are occasionally fizzy and come in varying degrees of sweetness—from dry to amabile (semisweet) to passito (fully sweet). My favorite maker is Fattoria Zerbina.

LAMBRUSCO

I hate to make blanket statements about wine, but lambrusco—the name of both a grape and a wine—is something I could very well do without. It's fizzy, sweet, and red, with a monotonous flavor of cooked fruit. The bubbles are put in the bottle using the Charmat bulk process—the same method used to put bubbles in soft drinks. I've read about old-fashioned lambruscos, made in the same way as champagne, but I've never encountered one.

SOUTHERN ITALY

Included in Italy's heel are the regions of Campania, Puglia (Apulia), Basilicata, and Calabria. In Apulia they make an interesting muscat, Moscato di Trani, sometimes called moscato reale. They also grow primitivo, which comes in both sweet and dry versions. You can also find aleatico both in natural and more alcoholic, fortified versions. In Calabria, Greco di Bianco can be found in both dry and sweet styles.

MOSCATO DI TRANI

This pale golden wine almost smells like a dry wine—no botrytis or caramel aromas—but once tasted reveals itself as off-dry, making it perfect for an aperitif or something to drink with fish or chicken. It's certainly too dry to serve as a dessert wine.

PRIMITIVO DI MANDURIA

Only recently, with the development of DNA testing, did we figure out that the primitivo grape is genetically identical to California's zinfandel, but you would never guess it by tasting the two together. Like California, where zinfandel is used to make both dry and sweet wines, in Apulia primitivo is sometimes picked late and used to make the port-like Primitivo di Manduria and other versions. I serve late-harvest primitivo (or late-harvest zinfandel) much as I do port, with an assortment of blue cheeses.

SICILY AND THE ISLANDS

Sicily's best-known wine, Marsala, may be the most underrated wine in the world. Unfortunately well-made examples are hard to find. Muscats pop up here and there, but the best known is Passito di Pantelleria made from zibibbo grapes, a variety of moscato, on the island of Pantelleria, which is closer to Tunisia than to Sicily. Another island, Lipari, is famous—as famous as an obscure island in the middle of the Mediterranean can be—for Malvasia delle Lipari.

MARSALA

It's hard to imagine that in the 19th century, Marsala was Italy's best-known wine. Nowadays we're unlikely to encounter it except as an ingredient in dishes such as zabaglione, where any finesse it may once have had is cooked off. Part of Marsala's fall from favor is due to a change in world tastes away from fortified wines such as Madeira (popular in America during the 18th and early 19th centuries) and sherry. Producers in Marsala—a town on Sicily's western coast—have done little to help its popularity by including inferior grape varieties, by sweetening the wine with boiled-down grape must, and by aging it in decrepit casks.

Three basic kinds of Marsala are named after colors: *oro, ambra,* and *rubino.* In addition to the colors, the amount of sugar in the wine is specified by calling the wine secco (driest but not completely dry), semi-secco, and dolce (sweet). To further complicate matters, Marsala is aged in cask for varying lengths of time. When labeled *fine,* it has aged for one year; *superiore,* two years; *superiore riserva,* four years; *vergine,* five years; and when labeled *vergine stravecchio,* it has aged for ten years.

If you want to taste a genuine Marsala as it was first intended, search out a vergine or vergine stravecchio. These wines are not only older, but the laws governing their production are stricter, ensuring high quality. Some vergine stravecchio wines are vintage-dated. If you spot a vintage Marsala, nab it—they're hard to find, and tasting a vintage is the only way to experience Marsala at its finest. Some of the top makers are Florio, Pellegrino, Rallo, and Marco De Bartoli, who makes a non-fortified version called Vecchio Samperi. Because Marsala is by definition a fortified wine, Vecchio Samperi is not allowed to have the word *Marsala* on the label and must be sold as a simple vino da tavola. When I'm lucky enough to get my hands on a bottle, I serve Marsala in the afternoon with a few cookies or Ladyfingers (see page 92). In the 19th century, it was served near the beginning of a meal with consommé.

ANCHOVY BRUSCHETTE

You either like anchovies or you don't—there seems to be no in-between. If you like anchovies, you're likely to love them, in which case this effortless hors d'oeuvre is well suited to an impromptu dinner or makes a good excuse to open a bottle of wine. I serve this with a light wine, such as Moscato d'Asti or a German Kabinett, a refreshing contrast to the piercing saltiness of the anchovies.

Makes 18 hors d'oeuvres (enough for 6 servings)

  1 **crusty baguette**
  2 **cloves garlic,** peeled
¼ **cup extra-virgin olive oil**
36 **bottled anchovy fillets packed in olive oil,** drained

Cut the baguette at an angle into 18 slices about ¼ inch thick—you'll have more baguette than you need—and spread them on a baking sheet. Turn on the broiler and toast the slices—watch them carefully and keep repositioning the baking sheet so they brown evenly. Turn the slices over and toast them on the other side. Rub the garlic on one side of the toasts. The toast is abrasive, so you can rub off a good bit of garlic on each slice. Brush the sides you rubbed with garlic with the extra-virgin olive oil and put two anchovy fillets, making an X, on each toast. Serve immediately.

TROPICAL FRUIT SOUP

Tropical fruits, vanilla, and ginger combine to form a vibrant yet delicate spiciness that goes well with sweet wines, especially vibrantly fruity muscats such as Muscat de Rivesaltes or Muscat de Beaumes-de-Venise.

Makes 6 servings

    2 **vanilla beans,** cut in half lengthwise
three $^1\!/_4$-inch-thick slices fresh ginger
    2 **star anises,** crushed
    2 **cardamom pods,** crushed
    $^1\!/_2$ **cup plus 2 tablespoons sugar**
    5 **cups water**
      juice of 1 orange (about $^1\!/_2$ cup)
    $^1\!/_2$ **teaspoon saffron threads,** soaked for 30 minutes
        in 1 tablespoon water
    1 **mango,** pitted and cut into $^3\!/_8$-inch dice
    2 **kiwis,** peeled and cut into $^3\!/_8$-inch dice
    1 **Hawaiian papaya,** peeled, seeded, and
        cut into $^3\!/_8$-inch dice
    1 **cup red berries such as raspberries, red currants,
        wild strawberries,** or **small strawberries**
    $^1\!/_2$ **pineapple,** peeled, cored, and cut into $^3\!/_8$-inch dice

Combine the vanilla beans, ginger, star anise, cardamom, sugar, water, and orange juice in a pot large enough to hold the soup. Bring the mixture to a slow simmer, cover the pot, and simmer for 5 minutes. Remove from heat and let cool. Remove the vanilla beans and reserve. Strain the mixture through a fine strainer, discarding the spices. Scrape the tiny seeds from the inside of each half of the vanilla beans and stir them into the strained syrup; discard the outer shells of the beans. Add the saffron and its soaking water to the strained liquid.

   Combine the fruits with the syrup in a mixing bowl and chill in the refrigerator for an hour. Serve in chilled bowls.

MALVASIA DELLE LIPARI

Before World War II, sweet malvasia-based wines were made throughout much of southern Italy. Of the few remaining, the best known is Malvasia delle Lipari, made on the volcanic Lipari Islands off the coast of Sicily. Malvasia delle Lipari comes in two forms, naturale and passito, both of which are sweet, but the passito is more so. For the less expensive naturale, the grapes are simply harvested when they are ripe; for the passito, the grapes are allowed to dry on the vine before being turned into wine.

The best-known makers of Malvasia delle Lipari are Carlo Hauner and Cantine Colosi. Wines from each have the characteristic aroma of malvasia—orange peels and nutmeg—and the Cantine Colosi naturale smells distinctly the way chocolate-covered maraschino cherries taste. There's not much difference between the Cantine Colosi naturale and passito wines, except that the passito is slightly more concentrated. Both have an agreeable taste of old wood and a good amount of acid. The wine from Carlo Hauner is fresher tasting and smelling and also lighter in color and less sweet. It smells and tastes of oranges and lavender. All of these wines are good in the afternoon with a little something sweet, as aperitifs with a few olives, or after dinner with a couple of dates.

MOSCATO DI PANTELLERIA

On the island of Pantelleria, the muscat of Alexandria grape—a higher-yielding variety known locally as zibibbo, with less finesse than muscat blanc à petit grains—is turned into two delicious sweet wines: regular Moscato di Pantelleria, made from ripe muscat grapes, and the sweeter and richer Moscato di Pantelleria passito, made from grapes turned partly to raisins on the vine. Moscato di Pantelleria may be fortified (and called *liquoroso* or sometimes *extra liquoroso*) or non-fortified. Passitos must be aged for six months in cask, and liquorosos for seven months. The best makers are Marco De Bartoli, Salvatore Murana, Cantine Colosi, Agricoli Sebaste, and Florio.

Above are three different Moscato di Pantelleria passitos. All share certain characteristics typical of passito wines. First, they taste of raisins, which makes sense since that's what they're made from, and all have an oxidized quality, which usually indicates that the wine has been aged in wood with some exposure to air and even to heat.

Unlike most Moscato di Pantelleria, which are made from muscat of Alexandria grapes, the example from Salvatore Murana is made from a variety of muscat called martingana. It tastes like Hawaiian papayas. Each of these wines is delicious with some firm hard cheese. A sharp English farmhouse cheddar is one of my favorites.

SAAR — RUWER
Grünhäuser
SPÄTLESE
Qualitätswein mit Prädikat Spätlese
Schubert'schen Schloßkellerei - D-54318
vormals Freiherr von Stumm-Halberg
8,0% BY VOL.
A. P. Nr. 3 536 014

Germany

German winemakers, more dramatically than in any other place, make wines that are both sweet and steely. German wines, while no longer really a bargain, are a boon for sweet wine lovers because virtually all—except a few reds and a few whites labeled *trocken* (dry)—are more or less sweet and are made in a style unmatched anywhere else. Their delicate sweetness is almost always balanced by an acidic core that makes these wines, even for those who claim not to like sweet wines, irresistible. I find them among the most delightful in the world.

Germany's greatest wines are from the riesling grape, but other grape varieties such as rieslaner (a cross of riesling and the higher-yielding sylvaner), gewürztraminer, pinot gris (called ruländer), scheurebe (another riesling and sylvaner hybrid), and huxelrebe also produce magnificent wines, albeit without the finesse of wines made from riesling. They can also be had for sometimes as little as a tenth the price of a comparable riesling, making them Germany's best bargains.

I suspect that the complicated labels on German wines are one of the reasons German wines are not more popular—long, unpronounceable words wrapping halfway around the bottle can be just too intimidating—but there's a simple logic to Germany's wine labeling system. A lot of information can be acquired with just a little knowledge. First, if you always buy wine with the words *Qualitätswein mit Prädikat* on the label, informing you that the wine was tasted by a panel of experts who attested to its quality, encountering a bad German wine is so difficult that even a stab in the dark means you're in for a treat.

German wine labels divide Germany into a manageable number of regions, and there are even different colored bottles that tip you off to the wine's basic style. Of Germany's wine regions, the most famous are the Rheingau and Mosel-Saar-Ruwer. Rheingau wines come in brown bottles and are made in a fuller, richer, and softer style than the wines of the Mosel-Saar-Ruwer. Wines from the Mosel (and two tributaries, the Saar and the Ruwer) come in green bottles, are leaner than wines from the Rheingau, and

Some of Germany's best wine bargains are made from grapes other than riesling. While riesling is the best-known and best-appreciated grape grown in Germany, we're so used to our German wine being made from riesling that we sometimes forget to look for it on the label and may accidentally buy something else.

I did this recently when I spotted this inexpensive (about a sixth the price of a riesling equivalent) Beerenauslese. It wasn't until I got home and studied the label that I realized it was made from huxelrebe grapes, not riesling.

Huxelrebe grapes are a hybrid that was "invented" in 1927 and are appreciated mostly for their high yields. While the wine shown below doesn't have quite the intensity, finesse, and elegance of riesling, it's a delicious, subtle wine with clean fruit flavors—green apples and underripe pears—and crisp acidity. It makes a magnificent aperitif.

have a nervous acidity that beautifully balances their delicate sweetness.

Lesser-known (which is not to say mediocre) regions include the Nahe, named after the Nahe River, which runs into the Rhine near where the Rheingau begins; the Pfalz (sometimes called Rheinpfalz or by its English name, the Palatinate), more likely to be planted with lesser-known grape varieties instead of riesling; and the Rheinhessen, which begins along the northern-facing banks of the Rhine, across the river from the Rheingau. These of course are very broad categories, but keep in mind that wines from the Nahe, Pfalz, and Rheinhessen are often a good value and are less expensive than the more prestigious Mosel-Saar-Ruwer and Rheingau wines.

Once you've scanned the label and found the general area where the wine comes from, there are several words that offer cues to the wine's quality and relative sweetness. Look for the word *Qualitätswein*, which appears on virtually every bottle of exported German wine. Qualitätswein alone indicates a wine of decent quality, not bad but lacking in the complexity and finesse of wine marked Qualitätswein mit Prädikat. Qualitätswein mit Prädikat assures you, among other things, that the wine can only contain natural sugar (lesser wines sometimes have sugar added before fermentation to make up for underripe grapes; see Chaptalization, page 18, for a description of this process). Germany's best wines always have these words on the label.

Once you've established that the wine in question is of high quality—it's labeled Qualitätswein mit Prädikat—you next need to determine when the grapes were harvested. Fortunately this is easy because German wines are all labeled consistently. To understand the labeling system, keep in mind that Germany's best wines are harvested at different times and that the richness of all levels of German wines is legally controlled with laws specifying the amount of sugar that must be present in the unfermented grape juice—called the must—before it is fermented into wine. A wine made from grapes picked during the first gathering, sometime in October, is labeled *Kabinett*. Most Kabinett wines have a relatively small amount of residual sugar and are the lightest of the mit Prädikat wines. Simply because they're made from the first harvest does not mean that Kabinett wines aren't of good quality—they can be magnificent. About a week after the first gathering, more grapes are harvested and used to make wine labeled *Spätlese*—meaning "late-harvest." Spätlese wines are usually slightly sweeter and fuller bodied than their Kabinett siblings.

After Spätlese comes *Auslese*, which means "selected harvest." The word *Auslese* appears on wines made from very ripe grapes that often have been attacked by botrytis. Auslese wines are almost always made somewhat sweet—when fermented to dryness, they're too alcoholic—and are often luscious and complex. After Auslese, and after a quantum leap in price, we enter the realm of the celestial. Weather permitting, a very late gathering of individual shriveled grapes is turned into *Beerenauslese*. And last, *Trockenbeerenauslese*, from the latest possible harvest, is made from individual botrytized and/or dried grapes, which is to say raisins or moldy raisins. Beerenauslese and Trockenbeerenauslese are very expensive, very sweet, and have surprisingly little alcohol because yeasts have a hard time thriving in a liquid containing so much sugar. Well-made examples contain an irresistible crisp acidity that makes these wines among the most delicious in the world. It takes a grape picker all day to pick enough grapes for a bottle of Beerenauslese or a half bottle of Trockenbeerenauslese.

It's easy to determine the general area—such as Pfalz or Reinhessen—that a German wine is from because it's identified on the label. After you've established the region, read the name of the wine. Except for a few vineyards whose quality has been recognized for centuries (such as Schloss Johannisberg and Schloss Vollrads), the first of two words is always based on the name of the town or village that the wine comes from. Eltviller, for example, means it comes from the town of Eltville in the Rheingau. Following the village name is either the name of the vineyard or of a larger area, called a *Grosslage* (the plural is *Grosslagen*). Wines with Grosslagen names are rarely of the quality of single-vineyard wines. Unfortunately the only way to know which is which is to memorize the better-known Grosslagen. A few of the more common Grosslagen wines are Zeller Schwarze Katz, Bernkasteler Badstube, Piesporter Michelsberg, Wiltinger Scharzberg, Bernkasteler Kurfürstlay, and Forster Mariengarten.

People often make the mistake of serving German Auslese wines with dessert, a combination that guarantees the wine will be overwhelmed. Beerenauslese and Trockenbeerenauslese can hold up to a not-too-sweet fruit dessert, but these wines are so special and expensive that I prefer to serve them alone or with a little hard, mild cheese. Kabinett, Spätlese, and Auslese wines make marvelous light aperitifs.

There are hundreds of winemakers in Germany, practically all of whom make more than acceptable wine, but for some of the top makers, see the list at left.

CHEESE PUFFS (GOUGÈRES)

These addictive little hors d'oeuvres are essentially cream puffs that have had cheese—I use authentic Italian reggiano or grana—worked into the batter before they are baked. Gougères should be served just before dinner with aperitifs, such as Kabinetts or Spätleses.

Makes about 40 small gougères (hors d'oeuvres for 6 to 8)

    1 **teaspoon softened butter** (for sheet pan)
1/4 **pound** (1 stick) **butter**
    1 **cup all-purpose flour**
    4 **eggs**
    2 **teaspoons Dijon mustard**
    1 **teaspoon salt** (for batter)
    1 **cup finely grated hard, well-aged Parmigiano-Reggiano, Grana Padano,** or **other very hard cheese such as aged Gouda**
    1 **large egg** (for egg wash)
    1 **teaspoon salt** (for egg wash)

Preheat the oven to 425°F.

Rub a sheet pan with the softened butter and stick it in the refrigerator. (If the pan isn't chilled, the dollops of batter won't adhere.)

Combine the 1/4 pound butter with a cup of water in a saucepan and bring to a simmer over medium heat. When the liquid is simmering and all the butter has melted, pour in the flour all at once and work it vigorously with a large wooden spoon, still over medium heat, until the batter holds together in a single mass and pulls away from the sides of the pan, about 1 minute.

Transfer the mixture to a mixing bowl and work in the eggs, one at a time, adding another one only after the previous one is completely incorporated. Add the last egg a half at a time, white first. Continue adding egg until a 1/2-inch-wide groove, made with a wooden spoon in the top of the batter, slowly closes in on itself. Work in the mustard, salt, and grated cheese.

Fit a pastry bag with a 1/2-inch tip and push part of the bag down into the tip, clogging it so none of the batter oozes out of the tip until you're ready to start piping. Make a 3-inch cuff with the top of the bag by folding down the sides. With your left hand, assuming you're right-handed, hold the bag open by slipping your fingers under the cuff. Using a spatula, fill the bag about two-thirds full with your right hand. Unfold the cuff and twist the top of the bag in a coil to seal it. Keep twisting until the bag no longer sags. Pull the tip away from the bag—unclogging it—and, while guiding the tip with your left hand and gently squeezing the bag with your right, pipe out small mounds (they'll have the shape of Hershey's Kisses) about 1 1/2 inches in diameter, an inch high, and about 1 1/2 inches apart (so when they puff they don't stick together); if you want larger gougères, make them 2 inches in diameter.

Beat the egg with the last teaspoon of salt until it darkens and becomes runny, about 30 seconds. With a small pastry brush (you can also use the back of a fork), pat the top of each of the puffs with a very thin layer of egg. (This also evens off the top of the puffs.)

Slide the sheet pan into the oven and bake for 20 minutes. Take a quick peek after 15 minutes (don't let the oven temperature fall or the gougères will deflate) to see that the puffs are browning evenly. If those on one end of the sheet pan are browning faster than the others, turn the sheet pan around. Turn the oven down to 300°F and bake for 10 minutes more, or until the gougères are well puffed and golden brown. Serve warm.

HOW TO READ A GERMAN
WINE LABEL

A. Varieta
B. Broad area
C. Vintage
D. Lateness of harvest
E. Village name
F. Vineyard name

GERMANY'S SEVEN MOST FAMOUS WINE-GROWING REGIONS

MOSEL

While usually thought of as a German river, the Mosel actually starts in France, in the Vosges Mountains, where it's called the Moselle. It then forms the border of Luxembourg and makes its way into Germany and eventually feeds into the Rhine, about 350 miles from its source. Unless you know your German wine villages, you may not know when you're drinking a Mosel, since wines from the Mosel all have the words Mosel-Saar-Ruwer on the labels, an unfortunate system that implies that wines from the Saar and Ruwer have the same style as those from the Mosel. But Mosel wines, while lean and racy compared to wines from other places, are full bodied compared to Saars and Ruwers. They couple great restraint with generous crisp clean fruit. Along with Saars and Ruwers, their tight acidic structure is unmatched by virtually all other wines in the world. To know whether the wine is a Mosel, a Saar, or a Ruwer, you have to remember the names of the villages.

Here are a few of the Mosel's most famous wine villages:
Piesport, Brauneberg, Bernkastel, Graach, Wehlen, Zeltingen, Erden, and Ürzig.

A

B. Nahe: This Nahe Auslese made by the respected winemaker Helmut Mathern has an aroma of caramelized pears and butterscotch. On the palate it tastes rich, soft, and inviting, especially when tasted next to the wines from the Saar and the Ruwer, which are so incredibly lean.

C. Pfalz: While most wine from the Pfalz is dry, there are marvelous examples of sweet wines, including Beerenauslese from Müller-Catoir. This wine is deep gold, with a nose so complexly layered with tropical fruit that it's practically hypnotic. On the palate it tastes like a combination of passion fruit and guavas. I must say, it is one of the most delicious wines I have ever tasted.

D

A. Mosel: This Mosel from Joh. Jos. Prüm, one of Germany's most respected winemakers, bears the name of Wehlener Sonnenuhr, one of the Mosel's most renowned vineyards. Wehlen is the name of the village, and Sonnenuhr the name of the vineyard.

This particular example, an Auslese, is somewhat light but has an intriguing nose that wine writers call "petroleum" and that reminds me of the smell of fuel oil in my furnace room. I also detect a hint of pine resin. Keep in mind that these kinds of associations, when subtle and integral to the wine, are not pejorative and in fact add to the wine's intrigue.

C

D. Rheingau: Rüdesheim, one of the Rheingau's villages, has particularly steep slopes for its vines. The wine shown here is somewhat light and relatively dry. It has an appley aroma that is strikingly austere for a sweet wine. You'd never guess this wine was sweet just by smelling it. On the palate it lacks acidity—especially compared with the wines from the Mosel, Saar, and Ruwer—but would make an excellent aperitif or a refreshing wine to drink with a hearty meal.

E. Rheinhessen: This Rheinhessen Trockenbeeren-Auslese from Nierstein is incredibly intense with floral and citrus aromas. It's intensely sweet, but with enough acidity that it remains refreshing. It tastes of exotic tropical fruits—fruits that may not exist or are yet to be discovered.

E

B

F. Ruwer: This Ruwer, a Spätlese from Maximin Grünhäus, (see photograph, page 60) is made by one of Germany's most respected winemakers, von Schubert. Especially for a Spätlese, the nose of this wine is astoundingly complex with layers of flowers and citrus fruits, especially grapefruit. On the palate it reminds me of a breeze coming off a field of wildflowers combined with a hint of lemon.

G. Saar: Scharzhofberger is one of the Saar's finest vineyards. There's nothing on the label of wine to tell you that it's from the Saar, as opposed to the Mosel or Ruwer, so you have to memorize the names of the villages, which is easy because there aren't many (see page 68). This particular wine, a Spätlese made by Vereinigte Hospitien, has an ineffable delicacy and the aroma and flavor of indefinable citrus fruits.

NAHE

The Nahe River runs into the Rhine near Rüdesheim near the end of the Rheingau. The wines from this relatively large region are hard to categorize, but they can be very fine. Their structure lies typically between that of a Rheingau—full bodied with less acidity—and a Mosel, which has a tighter structure and more acid. Because wines from the Nahe are less known than wines from other places, they are often a good value.

Here are some of the better-known villages:
Niederhausen, Schlossböckelheim, Meddersheim, Merxheim, Monzingen, Bad Kreuznach, Dorsheim, and Münster-Sarmsheim.

PFALZ

Sometimes called Rheinpfalz or Palatinate, this large area south of the Rheingau is Germany's second-largest wine-producing area. It has a relatively warm climate, and as a result, its wines often lack an essential acidity. Unlike in the Mosel-Saar-Ruwer and the Rheingau, riesling is not the predominant grape of the Pfalz; the higher-yielding Müller-Thurgau and sylvaner instead take the lead. There's a lot of inexpensive and indifferent wine made in the Pfalz, but if you limit your wine buying to mit Prädikat wines, you'll be assured of something very good for relatively little money.

Here are a few of the better-known villages:
Kallstadt, Ungstein, Bad Dürkheim, Wachenheim, Forst, Deidesheim, and Ruppertsberg.

RHEINGAU

The Rheingau is a small section of vineyards along the Rhine River that have the best exposure to the sun—critical for grapes grown in northerly areas. Wines from the Rheingau are the classic Rhine wines by which most other rieslings are gauged. Always sold in brown bottles, wines from this elite section are considered, along with those from Mosel-Saar-Ruwer, to be among the finest in Germany. In general, wines from the Rheingau are fleshier and richer with less acidity and a looser structure than those from the Mosel-Saar-Ruwer.

The Rheingau's most famous villages are:
Hochheim, Rauenthal, Kiedrich, Erbach, Hattenheim, Hallgarten, Winkel, Johannisberg, Rüdesheim, Schloss, Vollrads (not a village, but a very famous vineyard allowed to keep its original name).

RHEINHESSEN

This large area lacks the reputation of other regions in Germany, most likely because a lot of inexpensive wine, made from grapes other than riesling, is made here. Much of the wine made here ends up as Liebfraumilch, one of the reasons people think they don't like German wines. But mit Prädikat rieslings can be very fine and are usually a good value.

There are 167 villages in the Rheinhessen (120 of them end with "heim"), but here are a few of the stars:
Bingen, Bodenheim, Nierstein, Oppenheim, Dienheim, and Guntersblum.

RUWER

Of all Germany's wines, those from the Ruwer, a tributary of the Mosel, are the most strikingly elegant and austere. By some magic, they combine restraint and subtlety with forthright aromas and flavors. They also contain very little alcohol—usually around 9%—which makes them the least alcoholic of the world's fine wines. They are indeed among the world's finest wines and, while not cheap, are about a tenth the price of wines more widely recognized as among the world's greatest.

Here are some of the better villages:
Maximin Grünhäus, Eitelsbach, Kasel, Waldrach, and Avelsbach.

SAAR

This is my favorite of all Germany's wine regions. The Saar, also a tributary of the Mosel, produces wines with flinty and minerally qualities coupled with intense fruit. Because the valley formed by the Saar is shady and cold, Saars from off years can be just too acidic, but when they're great, they're truly great. To quote one of the great wine writers, Frank Schoonmaker: "[in good years] a certain number of [Saars] are, to my palate, the noblest and most remarkable white wines in the world." And for the time being, those of us who aren't millionaires can afford them!

Here are the best villages:
Kanzem, Wiltingen, Scharzhofberg, Oberemmel, Mennig, Ayl, Ockfen, Saarburg, and Serrig.

Two German wines, a Kabinett (left) and an Auslese, made by the renowned von Schubert family from Maximin Grünhäus, a village on the banks of the Ruwer River. Wines from the Ruwer are among the most beautifully balanced and understated of all German wines.

Most German wines are labeled with the village name followed by the vineyard name, but certain very prestigious wines such as Maximin Grünhäus are allowed to keep the original name as it existed before the laws were changed in 1971. On the label to the right of Grünhäuser (the er ending in Grünhäuser means "from") is the name of the vineyard—Herrenberg for both these wines.

GERMAN WINES:
THE DRIEST AND THE SWEETEST

TROCKEN WINES

While most Kabinett and Spätlese wines are vinified slightly sweet, dry wines labeled *trocken* are catching on in popularity. These wines will have the word *trocken* near the word *Kabinett*, *Spätlese*, or even *Auslese*. When shopping for a more or less sweet wine, it's easy to buy a trocken by mistake. Trocken wines contain more alcohol than sweeter versions because all the natural grape sugar is fermented, so the words *Kabinett*, *Spätlese*, and *Auslese* indicate the wine's alcohol content and intensity of flavor, instead of its sweetness. You may also encounter wines labeled halbtrocken ("halftrocken"), which means they are in between trocken wines and wines vinified in the traditional style.

EISWEIN

Made by crushing frozen grapes, *Fiswein*—known as icewine in Canada and ice wine everywhere else—has a very concentrated flavor because the water contained in the juice is allowed to freeze, leaving behind the flavorful components as liquids. When the grapes are pressed, only the most flavorful parts of the juice are extracted. This juice is then fermented into Eiswein.

German Eisweins are required to contain the same amount of sugar as Beerenauslese and tend to be very sweet but with a delightful, nervous acidity. Unlike Beerenauslese, which is made from late-harvest grapes, Eiswein can be made from grapes that haven't been attacked by botrytis. Even though Eiswein is very expensive, it's easier to make than Beerenauslese because it doesn't require the individual picking of botrytized grapes.

Ice wine is also made in other parts of the world, including Canada, where some especially fine examples are made and the sugar concentration is dictated by even stricter laws than those of Germany. (See pages 110 to 113 for more about Canadian icewines.) Some winemakers outside of Germany and Canada simulate authentic ice wine by putting grapes in a freezer and then crushing them. This technique rarely produces ice wines with the complexity of those made by letting the grapes freeze on the vine.

It's easy to tell from the label that this is from the Mosel-Saar-Ruwer—actually the names of three different rivers. To know which of the three rivers this wine comes from (each river location has a particular style), you have to know that the village of Ürzig is on the banks of the Mosel. This wine is in a brown bottle—unusual for wines from the Mosel, which are usually in green bottles.

CRISPY APPLE TART

This buttery and crispy apple tart is one of my favorites. I last served it with a Quarts de Chaumes, but any sweet chenin blanc or Sauternes-style wine would work.

Makes 8 dessert servings (one 13-inch-diameter round tart or 5-inch-wide rectangular tart)

For the tart:
one 14-ounce or 1-pound package **puff pastry made with butter** (available at most gourmet food shops)
 3 **Golden Delicious apples,** or more if the apples are smaller (1 1/2 pounds total weight)
1/2 **cup sugar**
1/4 **pound butter**

For the whipped cream:
 1 **cup heavy cream or crème fraîche**
 2 **tablespoons granulated sugar**
 1 **teaspoon vanilla extract**

Roll the dough out to between 1/16 and 1/8 inch thick. If the dough gets hard to roll or springs back after each roll, let it rest in the refrigerator for 30 minutes and roll some more. Don't force the dough to stretch when rolling or it will contract during cooking. Sprinkle a sheet pan with a tablespoon of cold water to help prevent the bottom of the tart from burning.

To make a circular tart, roll the dough out onto the sheet pan and place a pan lid or round pan with a 13-inch diameter on top of the dough. Cut around the edges with a chef's knife and pull away the excess pastry so you end up with a 13-inch-diameter round. Poke the dough in about 20 places with a fork to help prevent it from puffing under the apples. Refrigerate for 30 minutes.

Preheat the oven to 400°F.

Peel the apples, cut them in half vertically, cut out their cores with a paring knife or melon baller, and slice the halves crosswise as thinly as you can. Spread the slices, starting around the outside of the tart; each slice should overlap slightly.

Sprinkle the tart evenly with the 1/2 cup sugar and slice the stick of butter into about 15 slices. Distribute the butter slices evenly over the tart and bake for about 30 minutes until the apples are lightly browned. Because the pastry tends to puff, forming large blisters that disrupt your careful arrangement of the apples, check the tart every 10 minutes and use a thin-pronged fork or skewer to pop the blisters as they form and to nudge any apples back into their original arrangement. Don't worry if butter and sugar run off the side of the tart and burn—this is normal.

When the tart is done, let it cool for 10 minutes and slide a long metal spatula under it to detach it from the sheet pan (unless you use a nonstick sheet pan, the tart always sticks, but this isn't a problem). Transfer it to a work surface and, while gently lifting it one side at a time with the spatula, inspect it on the bottom. If there are any burnt patches—despite the sprinkling with water, there often are—scrape them off with a sharp knife.

Combine the cream, sugar, and vanilla in a mixing bowl and whip.

Serve the tart in wedges preferably while still warm (you can reheat it, but it's best served within hours of coming out of the oven). Pass the whipped cream at the table.

Note: To make a rectangular tart as shown in photograph, roll the dough out into a 5-inch-wide rectangle and arrange the apples in overlapping rows.

Portugal

While Portugal's dry wines have only recently begun to be appreciated abroad, Portugal's sweet wines—Madeira, Moscatel de Setúbal, and most of all, port, are renowned the world over. All three of these famous wines are fortified wines made by adding alcohol or brandy to the fermenting must to stop fermentation before all the sugar is turned into alcohol.

PORT

Many of us who know next to nothing about sweet wines are likely to have formed an opinion about port. I've never encountered anyone who doesn't like port, except when it's been served warm. Old-fashioned directions for warming the bottle of port next to the fire will only make the wine burn your nose. Port is best served at the temperature of a cool room or cellar—55° to 60°F—and if you're serving a vintage or late-bottled port (more about these later), the port should be carefully poured into a decanter so any sediment gets left behind in the bottle instead of ending up in your glass.

Like many fortified wines, port is more popular in other places—especially England, where it's been appreciated for 300 years—than where it is made. Don't ask what grapes are used to make port because there are over 80 varieties and often even the winemakers themselves don't know what they all are. Port, made along the Douro River upstream from the city of Oporto, is fermented in the same way as other fortified wines—by adding brandy to the fermenting must—and is made in four distinct styles. Port is one of the few wines for

which the grapes are still sometimes crushed by being trodden underfoot. The foot apparently doesn't crush the pits as does a mechanical press, pits that would otherwise release bitter compounds called phenolics into the wine.

Even though less than three percent of port is vintage port, it is vintage port we imagine sipping with Stilton and walnuts in front of a roaring fire. Vintage port is expensive in part because it is a blend of grapes from only the best parts of the vineyard, and also because not every year is a vintage year. In order for a maker of port to declare a vintage, the port must meet such high standards that there are usually no more than three vintages per decade. To compound matters, a vintage port takes a good 30 years to age even though the impatient among us have enjoyed many a younger example. Vintage port, like red wine, must be decanted (see Decanting, page 13) and drunk all at once, so there's no holding onto and savoring what's invariably an expensive bottle. Vintage port is aged for two years in wooden casks before being bottled.

Late-bottled vintage—sometimes called wood port or labeled LBV—isn't the same as regular vintage port. It's a less expensive port made from wine that's not quite good enough to be made into regular vintage port and is aged in cask for four to six years before it is bottled. This extra time in cask accelerates the aging of the port so it can be drunk younger. Traditional late-bottled vintage ports throw a sediment like regular vintage ports, but some more modern late-bottled ports are made with wine that has been heavily filtered, which makes it more stable and eliminates any eventual sediment (and a lot of flavor) so you don't have to decant it. The only way to tell the difference between traditional and modern versions is price—traditional versions are more expensive—and by checking for sediment if the bottle has a little age. Modern versions of late-bottled port are sometimes bottled with a twist-off cork (implying that it will be used more than once) instead of the traditional, extra-long wine cork used for vintage ports. Late-bottled vintage port can be drunk younger than regular vintage port because the extra time in wood softens the wine's tannins and makes the wine mature more quickly.

Ruby port is the least expensive port, bottled after two or three years in cask and filtered so it doesn't release any sediment. Because filtering port stabilizes it (and also robs it of some of its character), ruby port doesn't have to be drunk all at once in the same way as a vintage or traditional late-bottled vintage port. A good ruby port should have a robust, clean flavor and fragrance.

Like ruby port, tawny port can sit on the shelf to be drunk a glass or two at a time. Authentic tawny port, sometimes called aged tawny port, spends at least six and as many as 40 years in the cask, during which time it changes color from deep red—the color of ruby port—to a less opaque, brick color. Aged tawny port usually has the age stated on the bottle. Tawny ports are not vintage-dated, in part because they are often a blend of wines from different years. Less expensive, "fake" tawny port is made with thinner wine that mimics the effects of aging. Sometimes red port is combined with a small amount of white port to try to replicate the relatively pale color of tawny port. To identify an authentic aged tawny port, look for an age stated on the bottle and be prepared to pay a bit. "Fake" tawny port will be about the same price as ruby port.

When shopping for port, there are some other terms you're likely to encounter. The word *quinta*, which translates loosely as "wine farm," means that the port comes from a single section of a vineyard. There may be years when most of the port isn't considered good enough to be declared a vintage but in which a particular vineyard did especially well. In these circumstances, the wine will be bottled separately and sold as "quinta de something," like the Quinta do Infantado shown at right. Many of the major brands have their own favorite quintas.

Another somewhat unusual port is colheita, which is vintage tawny port. Remember that most tawny port has just the age on the bottle—it can even be a blend of wines from more than one vintage—but a colheita port will have the vintage on the bottle.

I serve tawny and ruby ports lightly chilled before dinner as an aperitif. If I'm stuck with a rather ordinary ruby port (I'm desperate and drinking the cooking wine), I pour it over ice and add a twist of lemon. Vintage, vintage-

Some makers market a "vintage-character" port—port that wasn't considered quite good enough to be made into vintage port, but that still showed character reminiscent of a vintage port. Vintage-character ports are usually aged in cask for four years (like late-bottled vintage ports) and can then be aged in the bottle.

style, and late-bottled vintage ports should be served after dinner. If I have a special bottle, I don't serve it after an elaborate dinner where there have been a lot of good wines, but instead serve a rather simple dinner so that people have plenty of appetite (and haven't had too much to drink) when I break out the cheese and port. I serve vintage port in the same large stem glasses I use for red wine.

Most port is sold by large makers who buy grapes from different vineyards and then bottle their port following their own traditional style. Some of the best and best-known makers are Graham, Niepoort, Quinta do Noval, Smith-Woodhouse, Taylor Fladgate, and Warre.

MADEIRA

Madeira is an island about 600 miles off the coast of Portugal whose fragile economy depends on tourism and winemaking. It's hard to imagine that this now obscure wine was once the drink of choice among American colonists. Until the middle of the 19th century, the United States was Madeira's most important export market, but during the late 19th and early 20th centuries, the combination of plant diseases, the Russian Revolution, and American Prohibition just about wiped Madeira out.

To further complicate matters, there's a lot of indifferent Madeira to be had; if you don't know what you're doing, you may wonder why you bothered tracking down a bottle. Traditional Madeira comes in four "flavors," each made from a different grape labeled clearly on the bottle. Madeira made from sercial or verdelho grapes is almost completely dry, with verdelho the sweeter of the two. Following in ascending order of sweetness are bual and malmsey (malvasia). Unfortunately a lot of Madeira is also made from an inferior red variety—tinta negra mole—that was planted after many of Madeira's vines were attacked by the phylloxera louse in the 19th century. Madeira made from tinta negra mole is labeled according to sweetness— dry (which is really off-dry), medium-dry, medium-sweet, and sweet—each level corresponding to the traditional grape used to make Madeira of that sweetness level. (For example, sweet is equivalent to malmsey, medium-sweet to bual, dry to sercial, etc.) The sweetness level is determined by when the winemaker adds the alcohol to the must—the earlier the sweeter.

Better Madeira is made using the same method that's used for most fortified wines—by adding alcohol or brandy to the fermenting grape juice before all the sugar is turned to alcohol—but lesser Madeira is made by fermenting the wine until it's dry, and then adding sweetener to the finished

Below is the oldest wine I've ever tasted. Very old vintage Madeiras are of course not cheap, but if you can find them, the price is manageable— a bottle costs about the same as a box seat at the opera.

This Madeira is almost indescribably complex, with a distinct aroma of wet cement underscored by the perfume of dates and figs, molasses, and an intriguing, vaguely petroleum aroma. On the palate this wine has an amazing amount of fresh acidity, so much in fact that while clearly old, it's hard to imagine this Madeira can be as old as it is.

Whenever I have a wine this special, I make it an event in itself and invite my best and most-appreciative friends. I serve this 1834 Madeira with firm-textured farmhouse cheeses.

STEAKS WITH PORT SAUCE

I still remember my first encounter with sweet wine sauces when, at about age ten, in an attempt to look sophisticated, I ordered beef tongue braised in Madeira. Sweet wines such as port, sherry, Marsala, Madeira, and Málaga all give a nutty complexity to sauces for red meats. If you don't want the calories, leave out the cream.

Makes 6 main-course servings

   6 **steaks, New York cut, strip,** or **tenderloin** (6 to 8
       ounces each)
     salt and pepper to taste
   3 **tablespoons olive oil**
   1 **shallot,** peeled and chopped fine
¾ **cup ruby** or **tawny port, Moscatel de Setúbal,**
       Madeira (malmsey), moscatel sherry, or
       Pedro Ximénez sherry
   1 **quart homemade broth,** without salt, simmered down
       to ½ cup (see Concentrated Broth, right), or **2 table-**
       spoons store-bought demi-glace or **glace de viande**
   1 **teaspoon crushed black peppercorns**
   1 **teaspoon red wine vinegar,** or more to taste
½ **cup heavy cream**

Season the steaks on both sides with salt and pepper and let them sit for a couple of hours.

Heat the olive oil in a sauté pan over high heat until it starts to smoke. Pat the steaks dry and gently put them in the pan by holding each steak on one end and then lowering it into the pan, away from you, so you don't get spattered with oil. Sauté the steaks, 3 to 7 minutes on each side.

When the steaks are well browned, transfer them to a platter, plates, or a cutting board (if you're carving) and keep them warm. Pour the fat out of the sauté pan and add the shallots. Stir the shallots around in the hot pan with a whisk or wooden spoon until you smell their fragrance, about 30 seconds. Pour in the port and boil it down over high heat until you're left with about ¼ cup.

Add the broth or demi-glace and adjust the consistency of the sauce by thinning it with broth or water or thickening it by boiling it down slightly. Lower the heat to medium, whisk in the heavy cream and boil down the sauce again until it has the consistency you like. If it gets too thick, thin it with a little more broth or water. Stir in the crushed peppercorns and the vinegar. Season to taste with salt and, if the sauce needs it, more vinegar. Spoon over the steaks.

CONCENTRATED BROTH

Homemade broth that has been simmered down to a thick syrup makes a delicious base for virtually any sauce for meat or poultry. When making it yourself, roast beef bones in a 400°F oven with onions, carrots, and celery for about an hour until everything is well browned but not burnt. Transfer the bones and vegetables to a pot, deglaze the pan, add enough water to cover, and simmer gently for about 12 hours, adding more water as necessary to make up for evaporation. Every 30 minutes or so, skim off fat and scum that floats to the surface and discard it.

When the broth is done, strain it into a clean pot and simmer it gently, again skimming off fat and scum until it reduces down to about one tenth its original volume, by which time it should have a syrupy consistency. You can store concentrated broth in the refrigerator for weeks and in the freezer for months.

Concentrated broth is now sold in most gourmet food shops or cooking supply stores. My favorite brand, which is also the easiest to find, is called Demi-glace Gold and is made by More-Than-Gourmet in Akron, Ohio.

GINGERBREAD CAKE

A glass of sweet wine makes a delicious accompaniment to an afternoon snack. If friends drop by and you offer sweet wine instead of tea or coffee, you'll be a major hit. A slice of this delicate and not-too-sweet ginger cake makes the perfect foil to a glass of sweet wine, especially a wine made in the oxidized style such as Madeira, moscatel sherry, or Moscatel de Setúbal.

Makes 6 servings

1 **teaspoon unsalted butter,** at room temperature (for the loaf pan)
1 **tablespoon flour** (for the loaf pan)
8 **tablespoons unsalted butter**
5 **tablespoons granulated sugar**
2 **large eggs**
¼ **cup molasses**
3 **tablespoons powdered ginger**
1 **teaspoon powdered cinnamon**
½ **teaspoon ground cloves**
½ **cup sour cream**
1 **cup flour**
1 **teaspoon baking soda**

Preheat the oven to 350°F.

Rub a 1½-quart loaf pan (mine is 8 inches long, 4 inches wide, and 2½ inches high) with a teaspoon of butter. Put a tablespoon of flour in the loaf pan and turn the pan to completely coat it.

Work the 8 tablespoons butter with the sugar using a wooden spoon or an electric mixer with a paddle blade. Work in the eggs one at a time, then add the molasses and the spices. Stir in the sour cream.

Sift the 1 cup flour with the baking soda and then gradually sift it a second time over the egg mixture while folding everything together with a rubber spatula. As soon as there are no more lumps of flour—don't over-work the mixture or the cake will be heavy—pour the mixture into the prepared loaf pan.

Bake until a knife inserted into the cake comes out clean—about 45 minutes. Let cool for 10 minutes, run a knife around the inside of the loaf pan, and place a plate face-down over the loaf pan. Holding the loaf pan firmly against the plate with a kitchen towel, turn the whole assembly over and give it a quick up and down shake to dislodge the cake.

wine. In times past, the best Madeira was sent in the holds of sailing ships to the West Indies and back again, the combination of heat and motion improving its character. Nowadays this effect is sometimes imitated by keeping the wine hot—about 120°F—for up to six months before it goes into cask, but this method is usually used only for lesser wines made from tinta negra mole. Madeira made from the traditional grape varieties is simply allowed to age while being exposed to the naturally changing temperatures (which aren't terribly extreme) of the island, usually for five to ten years but sometimes for well over a century.

Some of Madeira's best-known makers are Barbeito, Blandy's, Henriques & Henriques, and D'Oliveiras.

MOSCATEL DE SETÚBAL

The least known of Portugal's fortified sweet wines, high-quality Moscatel de Setúbal can be had at very reasonable prices. Don't confuse moscatel with muscadelle. Moscatel is simply Portuguese for muscat grapes (see page 130).

Moscatel de Setúbal is made like most fortified wines—alcohol or brandy is added to the fermenting grape juice—but the skins of the grape are left in contact with the juice for up to six months after the beginning of fermentation to impart a maximum of muscat flavor to the wine. Most Moscatel de Setúbal is sold after five years' aging in large oak casks, but it's worth searching out wine that's been aged for 20 years or more. Moscatel de Setúbal is made primarily from muscat of Alexandria but also from the higher quality muscat blanc à petits grains. A very small amount of red Moscatel de Setúbal—moscatel roxo—is also made. Most Moscatel de Setúbal is sold according to how many years it has spent in cask—usually 10, 20, and occasionally 40 years—rather than being vintage dated. Moscatel roxo, rare and expensive, is an exception and is sometimes sold with a vintage on the bottle and sometimes the age.

Moscatel de Setúbal can be intensely sweet and redolent of maple. I have a friend who likes to pour it over vanilla ice cream, but I prefer it with cheese such as Brin d'Amour, made from sheeps' milk.

COOKING WITH SWEET WINES

Unlike dry wines, whose depth of flavor is mostly lost when cooked, many sweet wines are so full bodied that they contribute real character to a sauce or braising liquid. It doesn't often occur to us that something sweet is delicious when juxtaposed with something savory.

You can make simple sauces using sweet wines as the base by sautéing meat or poultry, pouring out the fat, deglazing the pan with port, Madeira, or another sweet wine, and then whisking in a little concentrated broth and, if you like, a little cream.

You can also use sweet wines in stews or most dishes that involve cooking in a relatively small amount of liquid. Fortified wines such as Madeira, moscatel sherry, Marsala, and Málaga contribute not only sweetness but a complex nutty flavor that's a perfect backdrop for mushrooms (especially wild ones) and root vegetables such as turnips.

STILTON OR ROQUEFORT TART

Blue cheese tastes good with practically any sweet wine, but our most deep-seated association is with port, traditionally served with the English blue cheese, Stilton. If you serve this tart as a first course, serve a lighter style of port such as a ruby or aged tawny—the latter will be more interesting—instead of a vintage port, which would overwhelm any wine that follows. If you're serving the tart as a main course for a light meal or as an afternoon snack, try a cool but not cold tawny port or a Banyuls.

Makes 8 first-course or afternoon-snack servings, or 6 light main-course servings (one 10-inch tart)

- **2 pounds onions,** chopped
- **4 tablespoons butter**
- **1 recipe basic tart dough without the sugar** (recipe follows), prebaked as described
- 1/4 **pound Stilton** or **Roquefort,** broken into bean-size pieces
- 1/2 **cup heavy cream**
  salt and pepper to taste
- **1 large egg,** beaten

Preheat the oven to 350°F.

Cook the onions in the butter over medium to high heat—enough to soften them without browning—in a wide heavy-bottomed pot or sauté pan, about 25 minutes. Spread the onions evenly in the tart shell and arrange the pieces of Stilton or Roquefort on top. Season the cream to taste with salt and pepper—go easy on the salt, since the cheese is salty—and combine with the beaten egg. Pour the mixture in the tart shell. Bake for 30 minutes.

BASIC TART DOUGH

Makes enough dough for one 10-inch tart

- **1 stick** (1/4 pound) **unsalted butter**
- 1 3/4 **cups all-purpose bleached flour**
- **4 tablespoons granulated sugar** (omit for savory tarts)
- **1 large egg and 1 egg yolk,** right out of the refrigerator, beaten with a fork for 1 minute with 1/4 teaspoon salt
  pinch salt

Making the dough: Put the butter and flour in the freezer for about 20 minutes so they're very cold but not frozen. Cut the stick of butter lengthwise in quarters and then slice the sticks—keep them together in the original shape of the stick so you end up with 32 little cubes.

Combine the butter and flour in a mixing bowl or in the bowl of a food processor.

Hand method: Quickly work the dough by lifting it, a bit at a time, with the tips of your fingers and quickly crushing the butter into the flour. When you're done—don't do this for more than a minute—the dough should look like gravel with little if any loose flour. Add the sugar, if using, beaten egg, and pinch salt to the flour-and-butter mixture and quickly stir it around with your fingers—don't overwork it—until any loose flour is combined with the egg.

Dump the dough out onto a clean work surface and form it into a pile. Starting at the back of the pile, crush about a sixth of the dough with the heel of your hand and smear it backward, away from the rest of the pile. Continue in this way until you've crushed all the dough. If the dough is still crumbly, squeeze it together into another pile and repeat the crushing. You may need to crush the dough as many as three times to get it to come together. (Most recipes warn against this, but as long as the butter doesn't start to melt—in which case, put the dough in a bowl and back in the freezer—it isn't a problem.) Press the dough into a flat disk about ½ inch thick to chill it more quickly and make it easier to roll out into the shape of the tart pan. Wrap the dough in plastic wrap and refrigerate it for an hour before rolling it out. If you make it the day before, you may find the dough hard to roll out because it got too cold. To soften it, whack at it several times with the rolling pin.

Food processor method: Put all the ingredients in the food processor and process for about 30 seconds until the dough comes together in a ball.

Rolling out the tart dough: Start rolling out the dough by hammering the disk with the side of the rolling pin, then shape it into a circle about 13 inches across. Brush any excess flour off the dough—there are special brushes for this, but a quick swat with a towel does the trick—and roll the dough up on the rolling pin. Unroll the dough over the tart pan. Lift the dough hanging over the side of the pan straight up and press it into the corners of the pan with your fingers so the dough goes all the way up to the edge of the tart pan. Rotate the tart pan and continue until you've formed an edge in all the corners of the pan. At this point, use your fingers to push down on the dough against the rim of the tart pan so you cut away the excess dough, but push the dough in slightly from the outer edge so you have about ⅓ inch extra dough all around the tart to reinforce the sides and make them slightly thicker than the rest of the tart dough. Rotate the tart pan, pinching and cutting, until you've pinched all around the outside edge. With your thumb and forefinger, gently pinch and press straight down on the extra dough along the inside of the tart rim, making the sides slightly thicker and forming a smooth border that comes up a little less than ¼ inch above the rim of the tart pan. Chill the lined tart for 15 minutes in the fridge or freezer.

Prebaking the tart shell: When you're baking wet ingredients and liquids in a tart, you've got to cook the tart shell ahead of time or it won't ever get hot enough to crisp up. To prebake the pastry shell—what professionals call "cooking blind"—preheat the oven to 425°F. Cover the tart shell with a sheet of parchment paper with plenty of extra paper hanging over the sides so you'll be able to lift it out when it's hot. (Don't use wax paper, because the wax melts, and don't use aluminum foil, because it leaves little metal specks on the dough.) Fill the shell with rice or dried beans to keep the dough from rising up during baking. Bake the shell for about 15 minutes until you notice that the edge of the dough is matte instead of shiny and is colored a very pale blond. Gently lift off the parchment, doing your best to not spill the rice or beans, which you can save and use again. Bake the empty shell for about 20 minutes more until the inside loses its shiny, dull-gray look and turns matte and pale blond and the sides, which continue to cook, turn light brown.

Spain

Spain produces an enormous amount of wine, including many excellent dry whites and reds, but its most famous wine by far is sherry. Spain is also known for Málaga, a fortified sweet wine of enormous potential that when well made can be great. Unfortunately good examples are almost impossible to find.

SHERRY

Because there are so many indifferent substitutes, many of us think we don't like sherry. It is true that sherry has a completely different flavor than most other wines and is somewhat an acquired taste, but it's a taste worth having. Sherry has a lot to offer—subtlety, complexity, and sometimes intense flavor—and even the best sherries can be had for very little money. Sherry also makes a delicious aperitif or cheese wine. I even sometimes serve a slightly sweet sherry with main courses such as duck, game, or ham.

There are five basic kinds of sherry, three of which—*fino*, *palo cortado*, and *oloroso*—are made from the palomino fino grape and are dry. Two kinds of sweet sherry are made from the grapes that give them their names and are especially rich in sugar: moscatel (muscat) and Pedro Ximénez. Additional sweet sherries such as cream sherries or sweetened versions of oloroso or amontillado are made by combining varying amounts of Pedro Ximénez or moscatel sherry with dry sherry. To complicate matters, what you often get in a bottle labeled oloroso isn't just oloroso, but a sherry that's been sweetened. This is because the public associates the word *oloroso* with a wine that's somewhat sweet, whereas, in fact, genuine oloroso is bone-dry.

Most sherry is fortified with alcohol after it has fully fermented, producing a wine that's completely dry. Fino—made from the best juice of sherry's main grape, palomino—gets its character from a special kind of yeast called flor. Barrels of fino are kept less than full so that the flor can grow on top of the wine. When sherry was fermented in barrels—now most is fermented in

THE SOLERA SYSTEM

Once when clearing out a friend's garage, I came across a bottle of Madeira with 1909 on the label. When I finally opened it and swirled it expectantly in my glass, I found a rather ordinary wine. A little research explained my disillusionment—the wine wasn't from 1909. In fact, there was probably very little 1909 Madeira in it. Where did I go wrong?

In Jerez, Madeira, and other places where sweet wines are made, the wines are aged in a series of barrels called a solera. Old wine is drawn from the last barrel and partly replaced with wine from the barrel before it. Wine taken out of the second barrel is replaced with wine from the third and so on, with sometimes as many as nine barrels. The last barrel is topped off with new wine.

This system ensures that wines sold by a particular maker over the years maintain a consistent style and that some of the wine at least is as old as the solera itself. The year of the solera is the year this process started—not to be confused with a vintage wine. A wine carrying the date of the solera should be marked solera somewhere on the bottle.

Opposite: Here is a sweet sherry—PX—with one of France's tastiest cheeses, a Vacherin Mont d'Or.

stainless steel tanks—predicting which wines this magic flor would affect was largely left to chance. Nowadays the formation of the flor is encouraged by only lightly fortifying wines destined for fino—too much alcohol kills the flor—and using more alcohol in wines destined for oloroso, which by definition is never "attacked" by flor. Palo cortado starts out as fino—the growth of flor occurs on top of the wine—and is fortified accordingly. But then, the flor mysteriously dies and the wine starts behaving like an oloroso. Such wines are set aside in their own palo cortado soleras (see The Solera System, page 81). Palo cortado has a style in between fino and amontillado and is relatively rare and expensive. Like authentic fino and oloroso, true palo cortado is always dry. A true amontillado is a fino that's been aged in barrel for at least eight years, during which time the flor dies and the wine takes on its own character. A well-aged amontillado has a deep, rich nutty flavor that's magnificent with cheese. I like to sip on a slightly sweet version with a "Grilled" Aged Gouda Sandwich (see page 131).

So what do these dry sherries have to do with sweet sherries? First, most sweet sherries are made by blending sweet wine made from one of three grapes—palomino fino, moscatel, and Pedro Ximénez—into oloroso. The results are marketed under different names, but "cream" and "pale cream" sherries are the most popular. Some bottles marked amontillado are also sweetened with these sweet wines, although authentic amontillado is dry. The least expensive of these sweet wines used to make sweetened blends out of dry sherry is made from the palomino grape. Wines made from the moscatel (Spanish for muscat) grape and the Pedro Ximénez grape are used in the more expensive blends and are also sold on their own as sweet wines. Pedro Ximénez grapes produce an intensely sweet and dark wine that's almost like a liqueur. Traditionally, Pedro Ximénez wines were made with grapes that had been allowed to dry, but this is becoming unusual because using dried grapes is expensive. The very fine Pedro Ximénez from La Riva may be the sweetest wine I've ever tasted. It tastes just like incredibly good raisins but is so concentrated that I drink only a tablespoon or two at a time: once opened, a single bottle lasts me for months. When sipped with hard sharp cheese, its flavor changes strangely to chocolate. Moscatel sherry is very sweet but less so than Pedro Ximénez, making it considerably more palatable and more appropriate for most cheeses.

Some of the best sherry makers are Argueso, Barbadillo, Croft, Cuevas Jurado, La Riva, Osborne, and Pedro Domecq. Most sherry makers describe the flavor and sweetness of the wine on the label so that you don't accidentally buy an amontillado thinking it's dry, only to find out that it has been sweetened.

A WORD ABOUT GENERIC WINE NAMES

Inexpensive imitations of port, Madeira, and sherry are made in many places throughout the world in an attempt to foist off inexpensive wines—some of it undrinkable—as the real thing. While authentic sweet wines are never dirt cheap, most can be had for very little money.

It's better to buy an inexpensive bottle of the real thing than to waste money on something nominally cheaper and of far inferior quality. There are, however, exceptions, especially when dealing with port. Some very fine but fake tawny ports, such as the Australian d'Arenberg tawny are made in Australia and California.

Only two grapes, moscatel (muscat) and Pedro Ximénez, actually produce wines that are in themselves sweet. These grapes can be made into wine and bottled as they are, or they can be blended into dry sherries such as oloroso or amontillado to give them sweetness. These sherries are often called cream sherries, such as the one shown at left, from the excellent winemaker Lustau.

6 bone in chicken breasts
 salt and pepper to taste
3 tablespoons olive oil
1 medium onion, finely chopped
4 garlic cloves, finely chopped
1 teaspoon ground turmeric
2 tablespoons finely grated fresh ginger
1 teaspoon ground cinnamon
¼ teaspoon ground cloves
3 cups chicken broth
1 cup (½ pound) dried apricots, cut into ¼-inch dice
½ cup (¼ pound) raisins, preferably white
1 teaspoon saffron threads, soaked for 30 minutes
 in a tablespoon of water
½ cup slivered almonds, toasted in a 350°F oven for
 10 minutes until pale brown and fragrant

Season the chicken breasts with salt and pepper and brown them in the olive oil on both sides, about 7 minutes per side, in a sauté pan, preferably one with straight sides. Put the chicken on a plate and pour all but 1 tablespoon of the fat out of the pan. Cook the onion and garlic in the fat over medium heat for about 10 minutes. Stir in the turmeric, ginger, cinnamon, and cloves and cook for about 2 minutes more, still stirring, until you smell the spices. Pour in the chicken broth and all the remaining ingredients (include the saffron's soaking liquid) except the almonds. Put the chicken back in the pan, cover, and simmer very gently for about 10 minutes, until the thickest part of the breast springs back to the touch. Season the sauce to taste with salt and pepper.

Put the chicken in heated soup plates—the plates must have high rims because the sauce is runny—and spoon the sauce over it. Sprinkle with the almonds and serve.

CHICKEN TAGINE

Dried fruits and nuts give this Moroccan-inspired dish a delicate sweetness that works deliciously well with a sweet, but not too sweet, wine such as a late-harvest viognier. I like to serve this tagine with couscous, but rice will do in a pinch.

Makes 6 main-course servings

A LITTLE SHERRY VOCABULARY

AMONTILLADO: True amontillado is fino that's been aged longer than the usual six to nine years, sometimes as long as 40 years, in an amontillado solera. Like fino, amontillado is dry, except that some versions—some of which are very fine—are sweetened by being blended with a sweet sherry such as Pedro Ximénez or moscatel.

CREAM SHERRY: Winemakers blend dry sherries—usually oloroso—with sweet sherries made from moscatel or Pedro Ximénez. I find that moscatel sherries are generally better made and a better value.

FINO: Often made from free-run juice and the best grapes, fino sherry is produced when a yeastlike growth known as flor forms on the top of the wine in the barrel. True fino sherry is extremely dry. It is aged from six to nine years in cask before being bottled.

MOSCATEL: Moscatel (muscat) sherry is fortified *during* fermentation instead of after so that natural grape sugar remains in the wine. These are delicious sherries with nutty, dried-fruit complexity. Moscatel sherry is sometimes added to dry sherries to make cream sherries.

OLOROSO: Sherry wine that is not attacked by flor becomes oloroso, which is heavier and less delicate than fino, with a distinct flavor and aroma of raisins. Once it is clear to the winemaker that a particular barrel of wine is not going to grow flor, the wine is fortified to a higher level than for a fino to prevent the flor from growing later on. Like fino, true oloroso is very dry. Some olorosos are sweetened.

PALO CORTADO: A palo cortado sherry starts life as a fino—it's covered with flor—but then the flor mysteriously dies, and the wine starts behaving like an oloroso. When this happens, the wine is aged in a solera with other wines that have done the same thing. As you might suspect, Palo Cortado has the crispness of a fino but the nuttiness of an oloroso.

PEDRO XIMÉNEZ: A grape that produces intensely sweet, dark, and syrupy wine of the same name. It is sold alone or blended with dry sherry to make cream sherry.

SOLERA: See The Solera System, page 81.

MÁLAGA

Despite reading about Málaga in many a Victorian novel, until recently I'd never tasted one. My first sip, in a New York restaurant, struck me with its rich complexity and nuances of walnuts and maple. Tracking down a good bottle of Málaga isn't easy, and there are some that give away their mediocrity by a price below that of an inexpensive dry wine. But good Málaga—Scholtz Heuvanos makes the best—is worth looking for. Málaga is so rare today, it's hard to imagine that it was once one of the most popular wines in the world.

The main grape used to make Málaga is Pedro Ximénez, the same grape used to make very sweet sherry and as a sweetener for moderately sweet blended sherries such as cream sherry. Like sherry, Málaga is a fortified wine, but instead of waiting until all the sugar has been fermented into alcohol as when making sherry, brandy is added early in the fermentation, so a substantial amount of sugar stays in the wine. Málagas are naturally sweet, whereas sweet sherries are mostly made so by adding sweet wine (usually from Pedro Ximénez grapes) to fortified dry wine. And as though Pedro Ximénez grapes weren't sweet enough, in Málaga they lay the ripe grapes on mats and leave them out in the sun to concentrate the sugar even more. For some less expensive Málaga, unfermented grape juice is boiled down and added to the wine as a sweetener. Once alcohol or the concentrated grape juice has been added, the wine is transferred to casks for aging. Some producers use a solera system—look for the word on the label so you don't think you're buying a vintage wine (see The Solera System, page 81)—while others just leave each wine in its own cask. The best and sweetest Málaga is labeled *lágrima* and sometimes *trasañejo*, meaning that it's been aged longer than five years. Fine old Málagas are some of the most intensely sweet and complex wines in the world.

MONTILLA

People often confuse Montilla with sherry because the two wines are close to each other geographically and because they're made in a similar style. Unlike sherry, however, wines from Montilla aren't always fortified. There are three basic types: young fruity wines called *joven afrutado*, unfortified solera wines, and fortified solera wines called *generoso*. The afrutado wines are usually dry and so don't concern us here, but the solera wines are sometimes sweet. Once the wine has fermented—virtually all Montilla is made with pure Pedro Ximénez grapes—it is transferred to casks for aging. When making sherry, the wine is fortified at this point while the winemaker awaits the growth (or lack thereof) of flor. In Montilla, the wines have enough alcohol so that fortification is not required.

Like sherries, fully fermented (but not as yet fortified) Montillas are divided into finos or olorosos depending on whether flor has started to grow on top of the wine in the barrel. Both finos and olorosos, still unfortified, are then aged in their own soleras. Most Montilla finos and olorosos are sold without ever being fortified, but if either of these wines shows particularly good potential, the winemaker may decide to fortify the wine and allow the fino to age into an amontillado and the oloroso into a very special, aged oloroso. These wines are labeled generoso. Unfortified Montilla olorosos and finos are usually labeled dry, medium, or sweet and can be aged in a solera into very fine wines. Fortified Montilla is labeled fino, oloroso, or amontillado.

Montilla is hard enough to find that we usually can't be picky about the maker, but Gracia Hermanos, Compañia Vinicola del Sur, Delgado Hermanos, Pérez Barquero, and Toro Albalá are among the best.

DULCE MONASTRELL

Dulce Monastrell, shown above, is made from the monastrell grape, which is Spanish for mourvèdre, a deeply colored red wine grape planted widely in Spain (it's the second most planted variety after grenache) and in the south of France, best known as one of the grapes used to make red Bandol. Occasionally, mourvèdre is made into a sweet fortified wine by adding brandy or alcohol to the only partially fermented grape juice, in much the same way that the grenache grape is used to make sweet Rasteau and Cairanne. Despite being made from the same grape, this wine tastes nothing like Bandol; it smells very distinctly of black currants, with an aroma a little like that of concord grapes. It also has a delightful smokiness. On the palate it's sweet and round and invitingly fruity, with fewer of the wood notes we might expect in a glass of vintage or late-bottled port. Serve this wine with cheese or alone after dinner.

Hungary

Wine has been made in Hungary since Roman times, but it wasn't until the 17th century that Hungary's great wine Tokaji was discovered. As the story goes, because the region was under attack by the Turks, the harvesting of the grapes was delayed. When they finally got around to picking, the grapes were covered with mold. Desperate, they decided to use them anyway. The result was one of the world's great sweet wines and the first documented recognition of the importance of botrytis, the noble rot, later relied upon in winemaking regions around the world. By the 19th century, Tokaji wines were the darlings of royalty such that ordinary mortals couldn't even buy them. The tsars of Russia sent Cossacks out to the vineyards to guard them.

For much of the 20th century, the production and sale of Hungary's great sweet wines, Tokaji Aszú, Tokaji Eszencia, and the very rare Eszencia, were hampered by Soviet domination, but since the 1990s the quality has been improved and efforts are being made to restore it to its past glory. The Tokajhegyalja region, where Tokaji is made, is actually a rather large area—about 13,000 acres—that contains 28 villages including its namesake, the village of Tokaj. Only wine made in the area immediately surrounding the village is allowed to put the word *Tokaj* on the bottle; all others must say *Tokaji*.

Tokaji Aszú (pronounced toe-kah-gee oh-sue) is wine made like no other. Grapes withered and shrunk with botrytis are harvested in stages (requiring many trips to the vineyards, as in Sauternes) often into late November. Since the pure juice from aszú grapes (*aszú* just means the grapes are withered with botrytis—it's not the name of the grape) contains so much sugar that it barely ferments, if at all, the grapes are stored until a dry wine, called a base wine, is made. When this base wine is ready, the aszú grapes are worked into a paste and combined with the base wine. The paste was traditionally measured out in baskets, called *puttonyos*. The number of puttonyos added to a given amount of base wine—called dry Tokaji Szamorodni—determines the quality and sweetness of the finished wine. Tokaj wine may contain from three to seven puttonyos, with seven being extremely rare and made only in the best years. Tokaji Aszú with more than six puttonyos is

Opposite: I'm struck by the amount of acid that's contained in this wine, Chateau Pajzos 5 puttonyos 1993—enough to more than balance the rich caramel flavors of botrytis. There is also an undercurrent of not unpleasant bitterness and an oxidized quality that lies beneath. Tokaji wines often have an oxidized flavor because the base wine, which is dry, oxidizes very quickly. Don't serve this wine with anything too sweet. Grapes, preferably on the tart side, work well, as do firm mild cheeses, dates, and figs.

The wine makers at Chateau Pajzos have been experimenting with separately vinifying the three grapes used to make Tokaji Eszencia, then blending the wines so they have more control over the finished wine. One of these wines, the 1997 Muskotály shown above, has an intense and focused muskotály (muscat) aroma. It may be the finest muscat I've ever tasted.

labeled Tokaji Aszú Eszencia. No one actually uses the baskets anymore but, newer techniques produce the same effect with no loss in quality.

A small amount of the pure juice from the botrytized grapes is sold at fabulously high prices and is simply labeled Eszencia. It is the most expensive wine discussed in this book, costing even more than the 1834 Madeira. There's some disagreement as to how authentic Eszencia is made. Chateau Pajzos makes an Eszencia (shown at left, below) with about 5% alcohol, but the makers of Tokaji Stanza Eszencia (shown at left, below) insist that authentic Eszencia contains too much sugar for yeasts to grow at all. Amazingly, their Eszencia contains no alcohol. In addition to the levels of Tokaji, the three grape varieties—furmint, hárslevelü, and muskotály (muscat)—used to make Tokaji are vinified separately and sold increasingly under their individual names: Tokaji Furmint, Tokaji Hárslevelü, and Tokaji Muskotály.

Tokaji Aszú wines must be aged in casks for at least three years before being bottled. The best producers are Royal Tokaji Wine Company, Pajzos, Oremus, Disznókő, and Bodrog-Varhegy.

If you ever get your hands on a bottle of Eszencia, I suggest you save it for your grandchildren or drink it, drop by precious drop, all by itself or perhaps with a morsel of mild cheese.

BACON AND GRUYÈRE TART

I first enjoyed this tart in a restaurant in Manhattan that specializes in cheese. I was with a group of winemakers and writers who had gathered to taste some of the world's greatest wines, Hungarian Aszú and Aszú Eszencia. One of the evening's great surprises was a muscat, in Hungarian spelled *muskotály*, from one of Tokaji's most prestigious winemakers, Chateau Pajzos. It was one of the purest examples of muscat I had ever tasted—clean, fresh, direct, and focused.

To appreciate the greatness of such a wine, you and your guests need to distinguish what makes a muscat generic and what in particular makes this wine special. Now, unless I'm serving this wine to people who are already familiar with muscat in its many manifestations, I serve one or more other muscats, such as a Muscat de Beaumes-de-Venise, a Muscat de Rivesaltes, or for a really dramatic contrast, an Australian muscat shortly before, but overlapping with, the Hungarian masterpiece.

Makes 8 first-course or 6 light main-course servings
(one 10-inch tart)

2 **pounds onions,** chopped
4 **tablespoons butter**
½ **pound bacon,** cut crosswise into strips ¼ inch wide
   and about 1 inch long
1 **recipe basic tart dough without the sugar** (see recipe
   on page 78), prebaked as described
¼ **pound Gruyère,** grated (about 1 cup)
½ **cup heavy cream**
   salt and pepper to taste

Preheat the oven to 350°F.

Cook the onions in the butter over medium to high heat—enough to soften them without browning—in a wide, heavy-bottomed pot or sauté pan, about 25 minutes. Cook the bacon in a small, heavy-bottomed pan over medium heat until the strips barely turn crispy, about 15 minutes, stirring every minute or two. Spread the

onions evenly in the tart shell, sprinkle the bacon strips and grated cheese over them. Season the cream with salt and pepper and then pour it over the tart. Bake until the cheese is well melted, about 30 minutes.

Austria

Austria is still recovering from a scandal of the mid-1980s when certain producers were found to be doctoring their wine with harmless (but illegal) diethylene glycol. Fortunately the fallout from the scandal has brought about some of the world's strictest laws governing winemaking. Many of the same names encountered on German wine labels—Auslese, Beerenauslese, Trockenbeerenauslese—are found on bottles of Austrian wine, but the levels of sugar required by law are even higher. In general, I've found the wines impeccable, at least those I've drunk in the United States, and in fact among the best sweet wines I've ever tasted. The downside is that Austrian wines are expensive and hard to find.

Austrian wines also distinguish themselves from German wines by the variety of grapes used in their production. Unlike in Germany, where riesling (sometimes called rheinriesling in Austria) is responsible for most of the best wines, Austrian winemakers rely on a number of lesser-known grapes, such as scheurebe, which is a cross between riesling and the higher-yielding sylvaner; gewürztraminer (called simply traminer); welschriesling (a grape nothing like riesling that does splendidly well in Austria, though elsewhere it is used mostly for its high yield); and, surprisingly perhaps, pinot blanc and chardonnay.

Most of Austria's sweet wines, at least those that are exported, come from Burgenland in eastern Austria, almost in Hungary. Many of the vineyards surround the large lake Neusiedlersee, which provides plenty of moisture to encourage the growth of botrytis. Simplifying greatly, two styles of wine are made on the eastern and western sides of the lake. On the western shores, near the town of Rust, powerful wines with plenty of acidity as well as sugar are produced, while those wines made nearer the eastern shores, known as the Seewinkel, produce wines with a looser and less acidic structure that allows them to age more rapidly.

Other than Auslese, Beerenauslese, and Trockenbeerenauslese, Austrian winemakers around Rust also produce wine labeled Ausbruch, a distinctive style that was originally made by adding non-botrytized grapes to the must before fermentation, but nowadays is made from only botrytized grapes that are required to have a certain minimum sugar level. Depending on the winemaker, Ausbruchs sometimes have a slightly oxidized quality, but this is beginning to change as people prefer wines with fresher and brighter fruit. Ausbruch wines have a sweetness level between a Beerenauslese and a Trockenbeerenauslese.

Most of the Austrian sweet wines we find in the United States are made by Alois Kracher, who fortunately for us is also considered one of Austria's best winemakers. He's wildly experimental and makes an enormous variety of Beerenausleses and Trockenbeerenausleses, many from a combination of chardonnary and welschriesling. Kracher has his own idiosyncratic labeling system, reserving the words *Grand Cuvée* for his best wines; *Nouvelle Vague* for wines that have been aged in new oak casks; and *Zwischen den Seen*—which means "between the two lakes"—for wines that have been aged in older casks that impart little if any flavor to the wine.

A SELECTION OF ALOIS KRACHER'S WINES

A. Labeled simply #7, an intensely sweet Trockenbeeren-auslese made from a mixture of welschriesling and chardonnay. The wine is somewhat reminiscent of a Rheingau, which is to say that it lacks the steely acidity of wine from the Mosel but is much fleshier. Even though this wine is similar in structure to a German wine, it has a particular smokiness, perhaps from the chardonnay, all its own. Its aroma is very complex, with layers of flowers, citrus fruits, and butterscotch.

B. A Beerenauslese with no grape name, but I would guess that, like the others, it's made from a blend of chardonnay and welschriesling. As you might expect, it is less sweet than a Trockenbeerenauslese but has the same acidity, resulting in a wine that is beautifully balanced and still very complex, with an aroma that reminds me of caramelized tangerine peels.

C. Labeled #10, another Trockenbeerenauslese Grand Cuvée that's a perfectly balanced wine with plenty of lively acidity. It has a distinct aroma of grapefruit, which I encounter in many of Europe's finest sweet wines, especially those with a pronounced acidity.

D. Last, a Trockenbeerenauslese made from welschriesling, a grape I would never guess since this wine tastes to me almost exactly like a Sauternes (which of course is made with a blend of sémillon and sauvignon blanc).

LADYFINGERS (BISCUITS À LA CUILLER)

Those of you who have tasted ladyfingers out of a box will want to turn the page. But wait! Fresh-baked ladyfingers, served by themselves instead of as part of an elaborate, overly sweet concoction are delicious and delicate and perfect with a glass of sweet wine—a light way to finish a meal or as a perfect pick-me-up.

Despite their French name, which reminds us that they were originally formed with a spoon (*cuillière*), ladyfingers are nowadays piped out with a pastry bag. My own version of these cookies tends to be rather thick and large—more like plumbers' fingers—but you can make them any size you like. If you don't have a pastry bag, or if using one sounds too intimidating, you can spoon the batter as you would any cookie batter onto the sheet pans.

Makes about 35 ladyfingers

  5 **large eggs**
3/4 **cup superfine sugar**
3/4 **cup flour,** sifted onto a sheet of wax paper
     pinch cream of tartar, unless you're using a copper
        bowl for beating the whites
  1 **tablespoon softened butter**
  2 **tablespoons flour** (for coating the sheet pans)
3/4 **cup plus 1 tablespoon powdered sugar**

Preheat the oven to 375°F.

Separate the eggs into two bowls, one for the whites and one for the yolks. Put the whites directly in the bowl you plan to use for beating them; it should be large enough to fold the finished mixture.

Combine 1/4 cup of the superfine sugar with the egg yolks and stir the mixture with a small whisk until the sugar dissolves and the yolks turn pale. The yolks should be able to hold a ribbon for 4 seconds. Gently stir in 1/4 cup of the sifted flour. Stir just until the mixture is smooth. Don't overwork the flour or the mixture will be heavy.

Combine the egg whites with the cream of tartar (unless you're using a copper bowl) and beat the whites to stiff peaks in an electric mixer on high speed—usually about 1 1/2 minutes. Add the remaining 1/2 cup superfine sugar and beat for about 45 seconds more until the whites get very stiff and shiny. Taste a dollop of the meringue to make sure the sugar has dissolved and there's no hint of crunch. (If you're beating the egg whites by hand, count on 4 to 5 minutes of vigorous beating before adding the sugar and then 2 to 3 minutes more beating after adding the sugar.)

Pour the egg yolk mixture over the beaten whites— use a rubber spatula to get all the egg yolk mixture out of the bowl. Add half of the remaining sifted flour to the mixture and fold together, sliding the rubber spatula along the sides of the bowl all the way down to the bottom then lifting and folding the bottom over the top. Add the rest of the sifted flour to the mixture. Fold only until all the ingredients are evenly incorporated. Don't overwork the mixture.

Put a small dollop of the mixture in the four corners of two sheet pans and spread a sheet of parchment paper over the sheet pans, pressing it down on the dollops in the corners to hold it in place. Brush the parchment paper with the softened butter and put the 2 tablespoons of flour on one of the sheet pans. Shake the pan until the parchment paper is completely coated with flour and then dump the flour that doesn't cling into the second sheet pan. Shake it around in the same way. Hit the back of the sheet pans (work over a sink or large work surface) to get rid of excess flour.

Fit a pastry bag with a 1/2-inch tip, load it with the mixture, and pipe out the mixture in 4-inch-long strips, about 20 per sheet pan. While piping, hold the tip of the pastry bag about an inch above the surface of the sheet pan or you'll flatten out the ladyfingers. Hold a strainer over the ladyfingers, fill it with half the powdered sugar, and shake the sugar over the two sheet pans. If you're not using a pastry bag, use a spoon to dollop the batter on the baking sheet into ovals about 3 inches long and an inch wide. If you have trouble making the ovals, just make rounds.

Immediately slide the sheet pans in the oven. Check the ladyfingers after 8 minutes—they should be turning pale blond—and if necessary turn the sheet pans around or switch them with each other so the ladyfingers bake evenly. If the ladyfingers haven't turned pale blond, bake them for up to 2 minutes more. Let cool for 5 minutes then sprinkle them with the remaining confectioners' sugar. When the ladyfingers have cooled completely, take them off the sheet pan.

ROAST FIGS

While fresh figs make a perfect first course with a lightly sweet wine, at dessert we usually want something a little sweeter. Caramelizing the figs with sugar and butter is the perfect solution. I might serve this dish with a Monbazillac for a first course or with a Sauternes as dessert.

Makes 4 servings

12 **fresh ripe figs,** rinsed, immediately patted dry
 2 **tablespoons granulated sugar**
 4 **tablespoons unsalted butter**
 1 **cup crème fraîche** or **whipped cream**

Preheat the oven to 450°F.

Cut the figs in half vertically and arrange them flat side up in an oval gratin dish or baking dish. Sprinkle the sugar over and arrange the butter in thin slices on each fig. Bake for 45 minutes to an hour, until any liquid released by the figs caramelizes. Pass the crème fraîche at the table.

Greece

When most of us think of Greek wines, we think of retsina, the resin-flavored wine that's the standard drink at many a taverna. This is unfortunate, since we tend to ignore—or at least have trouble finding—Greece's lovely sweet wines, most made from muscat, either muscat blanc à petits grains or muscat of Alexandria.

The two best-known Greek sweet wines are Patras and Samos, which, at least when young, can be had for so little money that they may be the world's best sweet wine bargains. There is also Mavrodaphne, a grape grown around Patras in the 19th century by an expatriate German and maintained ever since. Each of these wines is both a kind of vin de paille (the grapes are dried-out off the vine before they're made into wine) and a fortified wine because alcohol is added to the wine before fermentation is complete. Those wines I've been fortunate enough to taste are made in a lightly oxidized style, with flavors of raisins and dried apricots.

Tasting two Greek wines together better reveals their flavor. These two wines, Mavrodaphne (left) and Samos, are distinctly different. The Mavrodaphne looks a little like a tawny port and is made in an oxidized style, while the Samos is fresher tasting and has an amazingly distinct flavor of Hawaiian papayas. Sweet wines are almost always enhanced by decanting, and the drama of a decanter filled with golden wine is hard to resist.

Moldavia

Now a part of Romania, Moldavia once produced Cotnari, which in the 19th century was rivaled only rivaled by Hungary's Tokaji Aszú and South Africa's Vin de Constance. Four grapes are used to make Cotnari: grasă for body and sugar, tămîioasă and frâncusa for acidity, and feteasca albă for aroma. Cotnari is said to be as aromatic as gewürztraminer and similar to muscat, but lacking in acid. I've never tasted a Cotnari, but I'm keeping my eyes out for a bottle.

United States

It's unfortunate that more sweet wines aren't made in the United States because some grape varieties—especially riesling—do very well when harvested late. Many American wines suffer from a lack of acid, but when wines are destined for sweet wines and are harvested late, the acid becomes concentrated at the same time as the sugar.

CALIFORNIA

Despite the popularity of California wines, relatively few winemakers make sweet wines. This is partly, no doubt, because of climate—it's often hard to get botrytis to take hold—but also because many consumers think they don't like sweet wine. It is interesting to note that until 1968, more sweet wine was made in California than dry wine. But that kind of sweet wine—for the most part, sickeningly sweet jug wines from the San Joaquin valley—is not what we're talking about here.

Winemaking in California is largely experimental because there has been less time than in Europe to figure out which grapes grow best in which places. As a result, a large number of winemakers, in all different parts of the state, are experimenting with different varietals and winemaking styles. Sweet wines are made throughout California, but a few of the better-known regions are discussed below.

ANDERSON VALLEY

Because so much of California's climate is hot, it's often difficult to make sweet wines that have enough acidity. Some winemakers add acid artificially, but in some places, especially those close to the sea like Anderson Valley, it is possible to make late-harvest and botrytized wines because there's plenty of fog to slow down ripening and encourage the growth of mold. My favorite wineries, where some of the best rieslings in California are made, are Greenwood Ridge Vineyards and Navarro Vineyards, both in the cool, foggy Anderson Valley. Joseph Phelps, though a Napa Valley winery, makes an excellent Anderson Valley riesling.

Navarro Vineyards is renowned for its late-harvest wines. These wines

FAVORITE CALIFORNIA RIESLINGS

These are three of my favorite California late-harvest rieslings (pictured opposite, left to right). It wasn't until I gathered these bottles and compared notes that I realized they all came from the Anderson Valley in Mendocino County. Any of these wines would make a delicious aperitif.

Greenwood Ridge Vineyards' Mendocino Ridge Late Harvest White Riesling: This wine's distinct citrus aroma reminds me of a Mosel— more than any other California wine I've ever smelled — though on the palate it is rounder and softer and makes me think of a Rheingau or Rheingau-style Auslese.

Navarro Vineyards' Late-Harvest Cluster Select White Riesling: The Navarro Vineyards' tasting room is right next to Greenwood's, so it's easy to hop from one to the other. This wine has distinct aromas like those of no other. I smell a pine and smokey aroma that reminds me of Christmas. On the palate the wine is sweet, rich, and round, reminiscent of a German Auslese or even Beerenauslese.

Joseph Phelps's Anderson Valley Late-Harvest Riesling: This wine is less sweet than the other two and seems to have more acidity, which makes me think that the grapes were picked a little bit sooner. The nose has a mineral quality that's very unusual in California wines. On the palate the wine is crisp, lemony, and refreshing.

are made in a fleshy German style—specifically that of the Rheingau—which is to say, much of the sugar is left in the wine; in Alsace, by comparison, more of the sugar, and perhaps all of it, would be allowed to ferment into alcohol.

A. The term "white" riesling comes from the days when California winemakers made "gray" and "emerald" riesling, using grapes that were different from the true riesling grown in Germany and Alsace. This wine, a late-harvest cluster select white riesling, has the characteristic flavors of botrytis—butterscotch and caramel—combined with apricots, a typical aroma in a ripe riesling. On the palate this wine is intensely sweet but with enough acid that it's not cloying. It makes a great stand-alone dessert.

B. This wine, labeled vineyard select, is less sweet than the wine to its left, but with plenty of apricot and less of the butterscotch aroma and flavor that signals botrytis. It's quite sweet—it has about the same amount of

sugar as a Beerenauslese—with bright flavors of citrus rind and grapefruit. I'd serve this wine with a not-too-sweet dessert like the Crispy Apple Tart on page 70.

C. This wine, labeled simply late-harvest, is reminiscent of a Spätlese or Auslese, with less of the flavor of apricot that's so typical of fleshier late-harvest rieslings. It would make a great aperitif.

THE AVA SYSTEM

Europeans have been making wine for millennia, but American winemaking has gone on for only a hundred years or so, with a hiatus caused by Prohibition. While France and Italy have long had laws designating winegrowing areas and regulating what kinds of grapes can be grown where, as well as the maximum yield a vineyard may produce and the time a wine must spend in barrel, American winemakers have only recently come up with a system of controlling and delineating particular areas, American Viticultural Area, or AVA, and helps wine buyers understand what they are buying.

As in the French system of *appellation contrôlée*, area boundaries go from larger to smaller such that a wine labeled American can come from anywhere in America and can even be a mixture of wines from more than one state. If only the name of the state is given, it is implied that the wine comes from more than one county within that state. A county name—the names of cities are not allowed—means that the grapes come from that county alone.

There are still many drawbacks to the AVA system, especially since winegrowing conditions such as soil and exposure do not necessarily conform to county or other limits.

MULLIGATAWNY SOUP

This Indian soup, originally invented for the English, who had a taste for foods mild rather than spicy, is a simple vegetable purée finished with heavy cream or coconut milk. Ghee (butter cooked until its milk solids caramelize) is stirred into the soup just before serving, which gives this soup an irresistible suave richness. Because ghee is full of calories, I give a range of amounts, so you can use just a little or throw caution to the wind.

Most people pair spicy, even mildly spicy, dishes with gewürztraminer, but I like sweet chenin blanc such as a Vouvray demi-sec or moelleux or Chappellet Winery's late-harvest chenin blanc.

Makes 6 first-course servings

- 1 **medium white onion**, sliced
- 3 **medium carrots**, peeled and sliced
- 4 **to 14 tablespoons unsalted butter**
- 6 **cups chicken broth**, or more as needed
- 1 **pound white cultivated mushrooms** (preferably cremini), rinsed
- one **14-ounce can unsweetened coconut milk** or 1 **cup heavy cream**
- 1 **tablespoon good-quality curry powder or**
  - ½ **teaspoon black mustard seeds**
  - 10 **curry leaves** (fresh, dried, or frozen) cut, at the last minute, into thin strips
  - 1 **dried mulato chile**, seeded, chopped fine
  - 1 **teaspoon ground cumin**
  - ¼ **teaspoon turmeric**
- **leaves from 1 small bunch cilantro**
- **salt and pepper to taste**
- ½ **teaspoon saffron threads**, soaked for 30 minutes in 1 tablespoon warm water (optional garnish)
- **lemon wedges**, for garnish

Put the onion and carrots in a pot with 2 tablespoons of the butter and cook over medium heat until softened, about 20 minutes. Add the chicken broth and gently simmer. Partially cover the pot and simmer for an additional 15 minutes. Add the mushrooms and simmer for 15 minutes more.

Purée the vegetable mixture 2 cups at a time in a blender. Start each batch by very quickly pulsing the blender set to low speed. Hold a towel around your hand and over the top of the blender to keep the hot liquid from shooting out. Use a ladle to work the puréed vegetable mixture through a fine-mesh strainer. Discard what doesn't go through. Stir the coconut milk or heavy cream into the soup; if you're making the optional garnish, save ⅓ cup of coconut milk or heavy cream.

To make the ghee, heat the remaining butter—between 2 and 12 tablespoons—in a heavy-bottomed saucepan over low to medium heat until it froths up and you see tiny specks of golden brown caramelized milk solids on the bottom of the pan. For a couple of tablespoons of butter, this takes about 30 seconds, but you'll need about 10 minutes for a half pound of butter.

As soon as the ghee is ready, set the saucepan in a bowl of cold water to keep it from burning. Stir the curry powder or mustard seeds from the spice mixture into the ghee and gently reheat it while stirring until you smell the curry powder's fragrance or until the mustard seeds begin to pop (about 1 minute). If you're using the spice mixture, stir in the rest of the ingredients and toast them in the ghee over medium heat for about 2 minutes. Immediately pour the ghee and curry into the soup. If you've used the spice mixture, strain the ghee into the soup to get rid of the pieces of curry leaf.

Stir the cilantro into the soup. Season the soup with salt and pepper and thin it if necessary with more chicken broth or water. Prepare the optional garnish by stirring the saffron and its soaking liquid into the reserved coconut milk or heavy cream. Ladle the soup into heated bowls and swirl about 1 tablespoon of the garnish on top of each one. Pass the lemon wedges at the table.

GOAT CHEESE SOUFFLÉS

Goat cheese is a little tricky to match with wine because it's relatively strong and can easily overwhelm most dry wines. Sweet wines, especially sweet wines made from chenin blanc, are the solution because they aren't too sweet to serve with these soufflés at the beginning of the meal, and they won't overwhelm the wines and foods that follow.

Vouvray is the perfect answer. A demi-sec is affordable and an excellent match, while a moelleux is magnificent but not always affordable. California late-harvest chenin blanc and not-too-sweet red wines such as late-harvest zinfandel and Banyuls are also a great match. If you're following the soufflés with a main course, choose something with which you can serve a robust red. If you follow a sweet wine with a timid red or white, it will taste too light or even thin.

Makes 6 individual first-course or light main-course servings

For lining the soufflé dishes:
1 tablespoon softened butter
6 tablespoons finely grated Parmigiano-Reggiano, Grana Padano, or flour

For the goat cheese base:
12 ounces full-flavored, medium-textured goat cheese
6 egg yolks

For the final folding:
10 egg whites
pinch salt
small pinch cream of tartar, unless you're using a copper bowl

Coating the dishes: Brush the insides of six 8- to 10-ounce soufflé dishes or custard cups with softened butter. Put the cheese or flour in the dishes and turn the dishes around until they're all coated. (Don't touch the insides after this point.) Put the dishes in the refrigerator.

Making the goat cheese base: Trim any moldy rind off the goat cheese and discard or nibble. In a mixing bowl, whisk together the yolks and goat cheese until the mixture is smooth, but don't worry about a little lump or two. Reserve.

Beating the egg whites, folding, and baking: Preheat the oven to 375°F.

Put the egg whites in a bowl with the salt and, unless you're using a copper bowl, the cream of tartar. Start beating slowly (slow speed on the mixer) and gradually increase speed. Beat the whites to stiff peaks, about 4 minutes with an electric mixer, 6 to 8 minutes by hand. Whisk about one-fourth of the egg whites into the goat cheese mixture to lighten it and make it easier to fold. Scoop the rest of the egg whites into the goat cheese mixture and fold it together with a rubber spatula. While sliding the spatula firmly against the sides of the bowl, reach down to the bottom of the bowl—where most of the heavier sauce base will have settled—and lift up the base, gently folding it over the whites. Continue in this way, cutting into the whites—but not pushing against them—as needed to combine the mixture. Don't overdo it—a few uncombined pieces of white are less of a problem than a heavy overworked mixture.

Gently pour the mixture into the soufflé dishes and place them on a sheet pan. Use your thumb to make a small moat around the outer edge of the soufflé mixture—this keeps the mixture from sticking to the mold as it rises. Slide the sheet pan into the oven. Bake the soufflés for 15 to 20 minutes until they rise by about 2 inches and are golden brown. Make sure your guests are all at the table. Move the sheet pan back and forth while closely watching the movement of the soufflé. If you notice the top rocking slightly back and forth, the soufflés aren't done. As soon as the soufflés appear firm, quickly place them on plates and serve them. Provide dinner forks or large spoons for your guests.

CENTRAL VALLEY

With its hot climate, the Central Valley is best known for jug wines and lesser wines used for blending. Quady Winery, however, has come out with some delicious and very inexpensive sweet wines.

MONTEREY

This viticultural area is much larger than the land surrounding the town of Monterey and in fact is divided into four separate zones: Monterey proper, Arroyo Seco, Carmel Valley, and Chalone (not to be confused with Chalone Vineyards). Most of these areas are dedicated to chardonnay, cabernet sauvignon, and some pinot blanc and pinot noir, but a handful of winemakers make late-harvest rieslings and gewürztraminers. Jekel is probably the best-known estate—their late-harvest riesling is quite good—but I've also found a delightful, not-too-sweet late-harvest gewürztraminer from Gan Eden.

NAPA VALLEY

Most of Napa Valley's wineries are devoted to making cabernet sauvignon and chardonnay, but a number of winemakers are experimenting with various forms of sweet wines, such as late-harvest riesling, gewürztraminer, and combinations of sémillon and sauvignon blanc. A few winemakers have even experimented with making ice wine. Napa Valley winemakers also make port-style wines by adding alcohol or brandy (sometimes brandy they distill themselves) to fermenting red wine. Zinfandel is especially popular for making port-style wines. A few of my favorite makers are Belo, Beringer, Far Niente (specifically their Dolce), Freemark Abbey, Grgich Hills, Robert Mondavi, Joseph Phelps, Prager (for their port-style wines), Pine Ridge, and Topaz.

RUSSIAN RIVER VALLEY

This region north of Sonoma Valley has two special wineries: Limerick Lane, the only winery I know to make wine out of furmint grapes (see page 126); and Arrowood, where they make an elegant riesling.

It's hard to imagine that the consensus in California was once that noble rot—botrytis—simply couldn't grow in the relatively dry climate. While not every winery makes botrytized wines, there are a surprising number that do. Here are five sauvignon blanc/sémillon blends that would give French Sauternes a run for the money. From left to right: Joseph Phelps's Delice; Topaz Wines' DLX (the top of their line, this is expensive; they also make a Special Select Late Harvest for less than half the price of the DLX); Robert Mondavi Winery's Sauvignon Blanc Botrytis; Belo's Sauvignon Blanc Dessert Wine; and, in front, Far Niente's Dolce (Dolce Winery).

SAUTÉED CHICKEN WITH SAFFRON, TOMATOES, AND GARLIC

This chicken dish uses some of the same flavors you might encounter in a Mediterranean fish stew or soup such as bouillabaisse. The garlic, though, is purposely kept on the tame side. I serve the chicken pieces over a small bed of creamed sorrel, but if you can't find sorrel, use spinach or serve some other vegetable on the side. Here it is paired with an Alsatian late-harvest (vendange tardive) pinot blanc from Charles Schleret, but late-harvest rieslings from other places also work well. Because this wine has a reserved varietal character, it makes a perfect wine to serve with food.

4 main-course servings

one 3- to 4-pound chicken, cut into 2 wings, 2 breasts, 2 legs (with the thighs attached), and the back
　salt and pepper to taste
　3 tablespoons butter
　4 tomatoes, peeled, seeded, and chopped
　1 small clove garlic, peeled, chopped, and crushed to a paste with a chef's knife
　½ teaspoon saffron threads, soaked for 20 minutes in 1 tablespoon water
　½ cup heavy cream
　4 servings creamed sorrel or **spinach** (optional)

Season the chicken parts on both sides with salt and pepper. Unless you need it to take up room in the sauté pan—when you sauté, the surface of the pan should be completely covered to prevent burning—discard the back. Brown the chicken parts in butter over medium to high heat for about 12 minutes on each side, until both sides are well browned and spring back to the touch. Reserve the chicken parts on a plate in a warm place.

Discard the fat in the pan and stir in the tomatoes, garlic, saffron with its soaking liquid, and the heavy cream. Simmer gently for 2 minutes and season to taste with salt and pepper. Serve the chicken in heated soup plates on top of or next to a small bed of sorrel or spinach, and ladle the sauce on top.

Left: Shown here are three of California's best viognier-based sweet wines: Andrew Murray Vineyards' Mon Amour 2000 (Santa Ynez Valley), J.C. Cellars' Late Harvest Viognier 2000 (Lodi), and Zaca Mesa Viognier 1997 (Santa Barbara County).

BERINGER VINEYARDS' NIGHTINGALE

Most winemakers in California make botrytized sweet wines when conditions are just right and the mold attacks the grapes in the vineyard. This means that many wineries don't produce a sweet wine every year.

But at Beringer, they actually grow their own botrytis in flat growing trays filled halfway with a gelatinous culture medium. After 10 days, when the mold has fully grown, it's diluted and sprayed on the picked grapes, which are arranged in racks. The grapes are covered and the room is maintained at 70°F and 100 percent humidity for 33 hours, by which time the grapes are covered with the mold. The grapes are allowed to dry slightly before they are pressed and fermented.

The result is a wine—a blend of sauvignon blanc and sémillon—with enormous depth and complexity and a distinct floral aroma that reminds me of gardenias.

A CALIFORNIA PORT TASTING

Some California winemakers produce port-like wines, often using the name *port* right on the label. Every one of these five ports is full-bodied and rife with ripe fruit. They're all delicious with cheese. My favorite combination is with a farmhouse cheddar from Vermont.

A. Sweet Leona: A late-harvest zinfandel from Linne Calodo in Paso Robles, central California, this wine has a distinct black pepper aroma underlined with the jamlike smell of ripe fruit. The peppery aroma is matched by a peppery flavor and a complex collection of cooked red berries.

B. Benziger's Port: This Sonoma Valley port is made of a blend of late-harvest Petite Sirah (not to be confused with the Syrah that's used in the northern Rhône Valley), zinfandel, tinta maria (one of the grapes used in Portugal to make authentic port), and tempranillo, a full-bodied, long-aging red grape that's used to make Spain's Rioja. The aroma is of roasted garlic and fresh mint. The flavor is of vanilla (probably from the barrel), chocolate, and coffee.

C. Montevina's Amador County Zinfandel Port: Amador County is in the Sierra Foothills and gets a lot of hot sunshine. This wine has an interesting aroma of the sea combined with strawberry jam. It has a delightfully peppery flavor.

D. Prager's 10 Year Old Tawny Port from the Napa Valley: This tawny-style port is the most reminiscent of Portuguese port. It has the typical (and delightful) aromas and flavors of roasted coffee, chocolate, and vanilla.

E. Domaine Charbay's Distillers' Port: This wine is made by adding four kinds of marc (grappa) and brandy, which are actually distilled on the estate, to partially fermented cabernet sauvignon and syrah grapes. It's so deeply colored that it's practically opaque. It tastes and smells of ripe berries but doesn't have the cooked jam quality of port-style wines from other, hotter places—the winery is on a cool ridge between Napa and Sonoma. While the flavors of this wine are different from Portuguese port, its buttery, long finish reminds me of that of a vintage port. It will clearly age for a long time.

PUFF PASTRY LEEK TART

This delicate crispy tart makes a great light lunch or an elegant first course. I serve it with something sweet yet crisp, such as a late-harvest riesling.

Makes 8 servings for a first course, light meal, or snack

- 8 medium leeks
- 4 tablespoons butter
- one 14-ounce or 1-pound package puff pastry made with butter (available at most gourmet food shops)
- 1 egg
-   pinch salt
- ½ cup heavy cream

Cut the greens and hairy root ends off the leeks and cut the whites in half down the middle. Hold the halves under cold running water to rinse out any grit or sand. Slice the leeks as thin as you can.

Heat the butter over medium heat in a heavy-bottomed pot and add the leeks. Stir the leeks every few minutes with a wooden spoon until they soften (bite into one; it shouldn't have any crunch left), about 25 minutes. Don't let them brown. Let the leeks cool.

Preheat the oven to 375°F.

Roll the puff pastry into a rectangle about 6½ inches wide and 17 inches long and between ¼ and ⅛ inch thick. Sprinkle a baking sheet with about 1 tablespoon of cold water. Roll the pastry up on the rolling pin and unroll it over the baking sheet. Use a sharp knife to cut off a ¼-inch-wide strip all around the tart. Cut quickly so you don't crimp the pastry.

Beat the egg with a pinch of salt and brush it on the tart. Be careful not to let any drip down over the edges or it will seal the pastry and keep it from rising. Poke the bottom of the tart with a fork to prevent it from puffing up too much. Spread the cool leek mixture over the tart, leaving a ¾-inch border uncovered. Bake the tart for 30 minutes, until the edges puff and brown.

When the tart has puffed and browned around the sides, bring the cream to a simmer in a saucepan. Spoon 4 tablespoons of the hot cream over the leeks. Bake for 5 minutes more and repeat with the rest of the cream. Check the tart every 10 minutes to make sure it isn't puffing in the middle and causing the leeks to slide off. If the tart is browning unevenly, turn the sheet pan around. If the dough starts to puff in the middle, poke the puffed parts with a sharp knife to immediately deflate them. Serve warm in slices.

SAN LUIS OBISPO COUNTY

A number of sweet wines are made in this section of central California, including the port-like zinfandel from Linne Calodo called Sweet Leona.

SANTA BARBARA COUNTY

Santa Barbara County, about 100 miles north of Los Angeles, is a large area that includes Santa Maria Valley and Santa Ynez Valley. Most of the region is best known for its pinot noir—which can be outstanding—and produces relatively little sweet wine. My favorite producers, and frankly the only ones I could find from this area, are Firestone Vineyard, with an excellent late-harvest riesling, and Ojai and Zaca Mesa Vineyards, both of which make excellent viognier.

SANTA CRUZ

This area south of San Jose derives its fame from the legendary Bonny Doon, whose experimental winemaker, Randall Grahm, will make wine out of just about anything. His best-known (and easiest to find) sweet wines are his Vin de Glacière and Moscato Fior d'Arancio, the latter an orange flower muscat. Ridge Vineyards also makes a late-harvest and botrytized zinfandel, though I have been unable to track it down.

SIERRA FOOTHILLS

This region is best known for its zinfandel. It's not surprising then that several makers produce late-harvest zinfandels, and one, Renwood, makes an "ice wine." I put *ice wine* in quotes because it isn't exactly authentic; the grapes are frozen in a freezer before they are crushed.

SONOMA VALLEY

Like Napa, Sonoma Valley gets a lot of sun, making it difficult to produce wines with the proper balance of acid and sugar. There are, however, a few glorious exceptions. My favorite wineries are Arrowood, Alderbrook, Benziger, Chalk Hill, and Ravenswood.

I recommend the following American muscats. Electra (shown above), from Quady, has only 4% alcohol. It's bursting with fruit and has good, refreshing acidity and a little spritz, a combination that makes me think of Italy's Moscato d'Asti. Like Moscato d'Asti, Electra makes an eminently drinkable aperitif. I serve it in the summer when I don't want everyone to overdo it before dinner's ready.

Considerably richer and more alcoholic (15%), the beautifully colored Elysium pictured at left is made from black muscat. The flavor is so fruity and so reminiscent of berries that it's hard to imagine it's actually made from grapes. I find this wine a bit too sweet to serve as an aperitif and instead offer it in the afternoon with a few cookies or Ladyfingers (see page 92).

Essensia, not shown, is again a sturdier creature than the Electra, with more fruit and more alcohol. It holds up well to a not-too-sweet dessert such as the Crispy Apple Tart on page 70. Essensia (no relation to Hungarian Eszencia) is made from orange muscat and indeed has an orange flavor.

A tasting of three late-harvest rieslings—one from California, one from Alsace, and one from Germany— is a quick and delicious lesson in how the winemaking styles of each place are different. Though you'll spend a lot for late-harvest Alsatian rieslings (vendange tardive) and even more for German Beerenauslese, the reward is great—you'll create an experience that will never be forgotten.

California late-harvest rieslings, for lack of a better comparison, are made more in the style of a German Rheingau than they are of a German Mosel—which is to say, rounder and softer, with less tangy acidity. Most California late-harvest rieslings remind me of apricots, again something they share with wines from the German Rheingau.

Alsatian wines are allowed to ferment more than their German equivalents, resulting in wines with more alcohol and a steely, mineral quality that German wines sometimes (but not always) lack. German late-harvest wines are only lightly fermented and often have amazingly low levels of alcohol.

Opposite: This muscat canelli—another name for muscat blanc à petits grains—has a delicate fruitiness that reminds me a little of a good-quality dark rum without, of course, so much alcohol.

NEW YORK STATE

Wines from New York State took a long time to establish themselves and gain a reputation for quality because earlier attempts and even successful ventures were made using the native American vine *Vitis lambrusca*. Wines made from lambrusca vines are often described as foxy. I'm not sure what this means exactly, because the only lambrusca wine I've tasted is Manischewitz, made from concord grapes. While not terribly exciting, it's not really bad either; it just tastes like grape juice with a little alcohol in it.

In any case, New York State wines are well ensconced, and New York is the third largest producer in the United States, behind California and Washington. While the tendency is the usual one of planting chardonnay and cabernet sauvignon, a number of winemakers in both the Finger Lakes district (far to the north near Canada) and Long Island grow riesling and make sweet wines, either late-harvest or ice wines. It would seem that winemakers in the Finger Lakes district could make ice wines comparable to those of Canada, but samples I've tasted, while good, aren't as good as a typical Canadian icewine.

OREGON AND WASHINGTON

Most of Oregon's wines come from the Willamette Valley, but as yet I've been unable to track down more than one Oregon sweet wine, a late-harvest riesling from Montinore Vineyards. Oregon has had the most dramatic success with pinot noir, but because of its latitude north of California, it would seem a logical place to grow riesling and make late-harvest versions of riesling and riesling-related hybrids. A certain amount of pinot gris is also grown in Oregon, such that the next obvious step would be a late-harvest version similar to an Alsatian vendange tardive or, even better, a sélection de grains nobles.

While Washington is the second largest wine producer in the country, its sweet wines are relatively hard to find, at least in New York. Chateau Ste. Michelle makes wonderful riesling, as does Hyatt Vineyards.

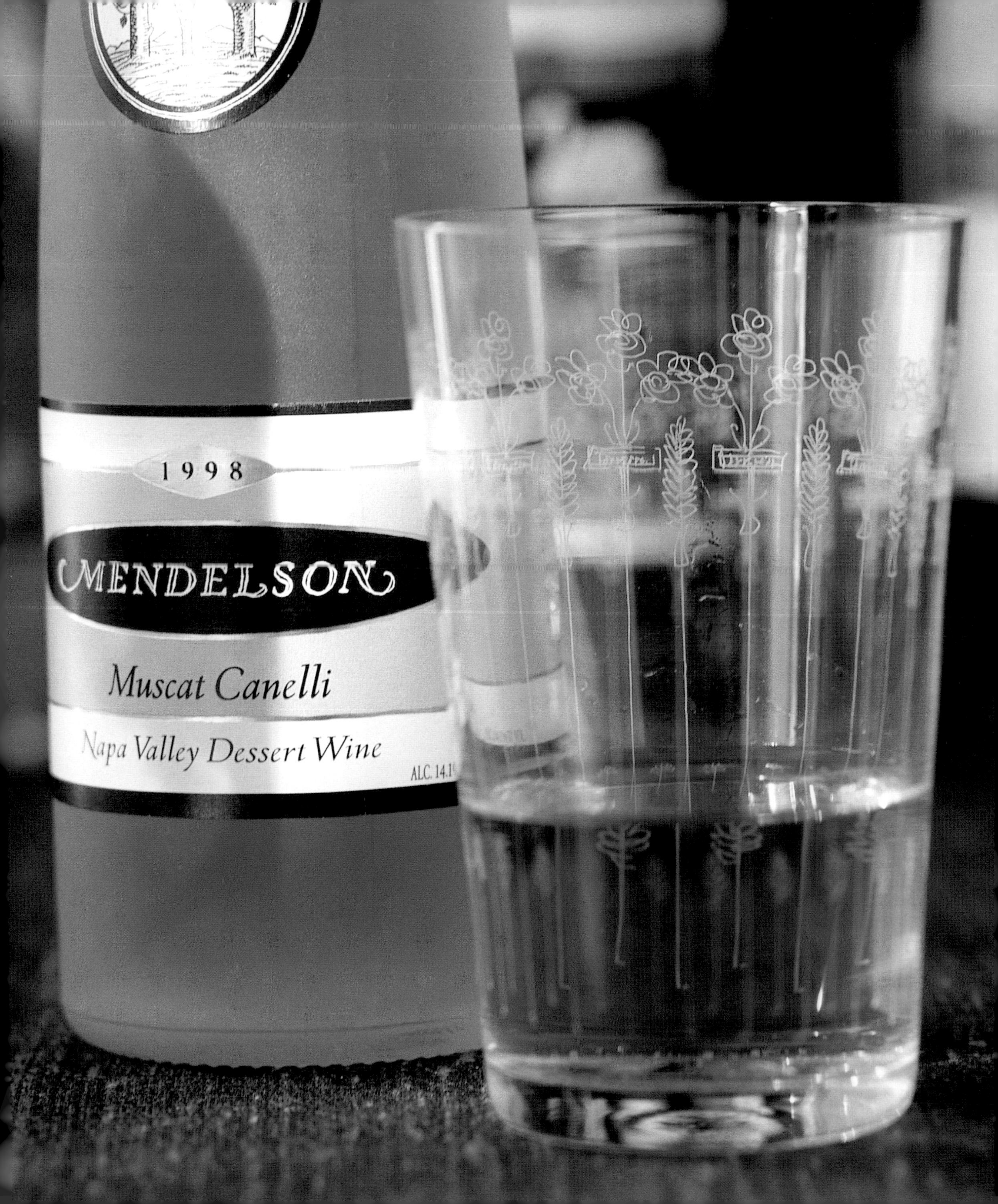
1998
MENDELSON
Muscat Canelli
Napa Valley Dessert Wine

Canada

Until relatively recently, winemaking in Canada was a dismal affair. Between prohibition laws similar to those in the United States, an arcane and onerous tax system, and the belief that only native grape varieties—such as the species *Vitis labrusca*—could survive the cold winters, it was close to impossible to produce fine wine. Fortunately, after World War II, this sorry state of affairs began to lighten somewhat as winemakers started experimenting with European varietals, or, more precisely, European varietals that had been grafted onto native American rootstocks, a solution used in Europe to outfox the phylloxera louse that devastated most of Europe's vineyards in the late 19th century.

Most exciting has been the development, in the late 1970s, of Canadian icewines made by crushing frozen grapes (see Eiswein, page 69) that then release a sweet syrupy elixir. Because 70 to 80 percent of the grape juice is lost in the production process, the cost of making icewine is obviously very high, but so is the payoff: Canadian icewines are some of the finest sweet wines in the world. While the Germans have been making icewine—Eiswein—for centuries, most wine-growing regions, especially in the New World, don't have the warm summers and cold autumns that are needed to allow the grapes to ripen and then freeze. And it isn't a simple matter of freezing the harvested grapes. Canadian laws—among the most rigorous in the world—require that the grapes not be picked until temperatures are well below freezing, so there's less chance of the frozen juice melting while being pressed. The long growing season coupled with gentle summers allows the grapes to develop flavor and, perhaps most important, to retain enough natural acid to balance the intense sweetness of the finished icewine.

What's most exciting is the number of icewines (spelled *ice wine* in other non-German places) that Canadian winemakers produce. No grape variety puts them off, leaving them to produce aromatic and fascinating wines from unlikely grapes. Chardonnay icewine is stunningly delicious (see page 124 for a comparison of late-harvest and icewine chardonnays), as are chenin blanc, merlot, cabernet franc,

THE VQA SYSTEM

The VQA—Vintners Quality Alliance—was formed in the 1980s to bring some order to the labeling of Canadian wines. Since its formation, the VQA has imposed some of the strictest winemaking rules in the world.

Most of the time, 100 percent of the grapes must be from the area designated on the label and must be presented to a panel of tasters who deny the winemaker the VQA label if the wine doesn't meet certain standards. Sometimes the number of rejected applicants approaches 50 percent!

Minimum sugar contents are stipulated for certain designations. Remember that 1 degree Brix equals 18 grams of sugar per liter (see Potential Alcohol and Residual Sugar, page 19). To get a sense of what that means, German and Austrian Eisweins must contain 28.5 degrees Brix, and 29 degrees Brix, respectively.

Here are the required sugar levels for Canadian sweet wines: Late Harvest (22° Brix), Select Late Harvest (26° Brix), Botrytis Affected (BA 26° Brix), Special Select Late Harvest (30° Brix), Totally Botrytis Affected (TBA 34° Brix), and Icewine (35° Brix).

Left: Inniskillin, an Ontario-based maker, is one of Canada's best-known producers of icewines, including vidal, oak-aged vidal, chenin blanc (very unusual), cabernet franc, and riesling.

FRENCH ONION SOUP

Good French onion soup can be so sweet from the natural sugar contained in the onions that it sometimes interferes with a red wine. I like it with a sweet Madeira (ideally an old Malmsey) or sherry, a Moscatel de Setúbal, a ruby or tawny port, or a Rivesaltes ambré. I'd also suggest "M" from Cedar-Creek, a Canadian Madeira look-alike.

Makes 10 first-course servings

   5 **pounds onions**
   4 **tablespoons butter**
 10 **cups beef, turkey, or chicken broth**
      bouquet garni (3 sprigs thyme, 3 sprigs parsley, and 1 bay leaf tied together with a piece of string)
      salt and pepper to taste
   2 **cups finely grated Swiss Gruyère** (about ½ pound)
 10 **thick slices French bread,** cut from a large loaf and toasted

In advance: Peel and slice the onions as finely as you can. Melt the butter in a wide, heavy-bottomed 4-quart pot and add the onions. Stir the onions every few minutes over medium heat until they soften and begin to brown, about 40 minutes. When they start to brown, pour in ½ cup of broth and turn the heat on high. Stir the onions, scraping off any caramelized juices that have clung to the bottom and sides of the pan. When the broth has completely evaporated and forms a brown glaze on the bottom of the pan, add another ½ cup of broth and repeat. Continue doing this until you've used up 2 cups of the broth.

Add the remaining broth and the bouquet garni to the onions and gently simmer the soup for 15 minutes. Be sure to scrape the pan so the caramelized juices dissolve in the soup. Season with salt and pepper. Remove the bouquet garni.

Last minute: Preheat the oven to 400°F. Ladle the hot soup into deep, ovenproof bowls. Sprinkle half the cheese over the soup and place a slice of toast on each one. Sprinkle with the remaining cheese. Put the bowls on a sheet pan and bake them in the oven until the cheese bubbles and turns light brown, about 10 minutes.

3 boneless Pekin (Long Island) duck breasts, 1 boneless mullard duck breast or 3 boneless chicken
breasts (total weight about 1 pound)

1 cup sake

$\frac{1}{3}$ cup soy sauce

4 tablespoons sugar

$\frac{1}{2}$ teaspoon dark Asian sesame oil (preferably a
Japanese brand)

2 tablespoons sesame seeds, toasted lightly in a heavy
skillet for about 3 minutes until they are fragrant

Take the skin off the duck or chicken breasts and cut the meat into approximately $\frac{2}{3}$-inch squares.

Combine the rest of the ingredients except the sesame seeds in a small saucepan and boil the mixture down to about half until it becomes syrupy. Let cool. Reserve 3 tablespoons of the mixture for brushing on the kebabs. Stir the meat into the cooled glaze and let marinate for 4 hours.

Thread the squares of duck breast on skewers. If you use wooden skewers, make sure there's no space between the squares of meat and wrap the ends in aluminum foil or the wood will burn. Grill the skewers over very hot coals or in a preheated grill pan for 3 minutes on the first side and 2 minutes on the second. If you're grilling outside or have a hood in the kitchen, use the reserved liquid to brush on the kebabs a minute or so before they have finished cooking. If you don't have a hood and are grilling inside, skip the brushing or you'll smoke up the kitchen. Sprinkle the sesame seeds over the kebabs while rotating the skewers and grill for 30 seconds more. Serve on hot plates.

DUCK OR CHICKEN YAKITORI

These savory little kebabs can be made from virtually any meat, firm fish, or shellfish, and vegetables. Duck is my favorite (mullards, large ducks with flavorful and meaty breasts, are especially good); chicken is a close second. These are delicious served as a first course or hors d'oeuvre with a moderately sweet wine. Gehringer Brothers Schönburger from British Columbia is perfect.

Makes 4 hors d'oeuvre or light first-course servings

riesling (probably the best), and a large number of German hybrids such as kerner, optima, vidal, and ehrenfelser. Some winemakers—Inniskillin in Ontario and Jackson-Triggs, now with a foothold in British Columbia in addition to their Ontario-based facilities—even make sparkling icewine rieslings in which the bubbles seem suspended in icy tangy fruit. They're among the most luxurious drinks to be had. Because the laws governing the production of Canadian icewine are so strict (see VQA, page 110), it's difficult for a winemaker to cheat and resort to tricks such as adding sugar to the wine or freezing the grapes artificially, a method that produces less flavorful wine.

ONTARIO

The best-known Canadian icewines come from Ontario. While I've never tasted a bad icewine, a few makers stand out: Inniskillin, Château des Charmes, Reif, Hillebrand, Jackson-Triggs, D'Angelo, Gehringer Brothers, Henry of Pelham, and Pillitteri.

BRITISH COLUMBIA

Wines from British Columbia can be hard to track down, especially on the East Coast of the United States where I live, and had it not been for a recent tasting, I might never have known they were there. But what a revelation!

Here are some of my favorite makers:
Quails' Gate, Mt. Boucherie, Red Rooster, Mission Hill, Gray Monk, Calona Vineyards, Paradise Ranch, Lang Vineyards, Domaine Combret, St. Hubertus, Black Hills, Tinhorn Creek, Sumac Ridge, Hawthorne Mountain Vineyards.

Above left: An assortment of excellent sweet wines from British Columbia.

PIRRAMIMMA

McLaren Vale

1998

late harvest

riesling

HENSCHKE

Noble

EDEN

PRODUCE OF AUSTRALIA

WINE CHALLENGE 1999 GOLD

WINPAC HONG KONG 1998 GOLD

SILVER AWARD SILVER

WINE CHALLENGE SILVER

d'Arenberg

EST. 1912

THE NOBLE

RIESLING

McLAREN VALE

Australia

A number of stunningly delicious fortified sweet wines are made in Australia. Among them is liqueur tokay, a golden, sweet, nutty wine reminiscent of very sweet Madeira, usually made from the muscadelle grape (not to be confused with muscat or muscadet or other wines called tokay; see What Is Tokay? on page 129) but sometimes with pinot gris. The aroma of liqueur tokay reminds me, oddly but very pleasantly, of olives. While these wines are too sweet to serve as aperitifs, they're great in the afternoon with a couple of cookies or alone, after dinner. Liqueur muscat is made from a variety of muscat blanc à petits grains, in Australia called brown muscat. The wine is deep brown in the glass—and tastes (and looks) like maple syrup.

All of Australia's liqueur wines are fortified wines, made by adding brandy or alcohol to the partially fermented must that is then allowed to oxidize by being placed in the sun in not-quite-full barrels. Australia's fortified wines are rarely vintage-dated but are likely to carry the words *classic*, *grand*, or *rare*—words used in ascending order to describe richness, age, and rarity. Older vintages may be marked, following an older system, with the word *special*. Most of Australia's fortified wines, including some very special port-like wines, are made using the solera system (see The Solera System, page 81), resulting in blends that contain some very old wines for complexity and young wines for freshness.

A number of botrytized wines are also made in Australia, including Yalumba Winery's botrytized semillon. While it doesn't taste like Sauternes as you might expect (the grapes are the same), it is a very fine wine in its own right, with a distinct but not unpleasant woody flavor and a sprightly acidity. Its aroma reminds me of bourbon and fenugreek, one of the main spices used in curry powder and for flavoring artificial maple syrup. Late-harvest rieslings are also very successful in Australia (see photograph, opposite).

Some of Australia's most reputable makers of sweet wines include All Saints, Baileys, Bridges, Brown Brothers, Campbell's, Chambers, d'Arenberg, Henschke, Morris, Peter Lehmann, Penfolds, Pirramimma, Seppelt, and Yalumba.

Opposite. Here are three Australian rieslings. The 1998 late-harvest riesling from Pirramimma, in McLaren Vale township, is paler, less sweet, and less complex than (and half the price of) the riesling from d'Arenberg shown at right. It's comparable to a German Auslese but without the same finesse, and it can be had for much less.

Henschke's 1999 Noble Rot Riesling is pale orange and has a distinct aroma and flavor of apricots—or, more precisely, apricot jam. It makes me think of a riesling from the Rheingau but without quite the elegance and without as much acid. It's comparable in sweetness to a Beerenauslese.

D'Arenberg's 1997 "The Noble," also made in McLaren Vale, is deep orange and has about the same sweetness as a German Beerenauslese. It contains a good amount of acid (if not that of a well-made Beerenauslese) to balance its sweetness and a welcome hint of oak that adds to its complexity. While not inexpensive, this wine is a good value—about a third the price of a comparable German wine.

Below: Usually I don't recommend wines that are trying to be something else, but this "Rare Tawny" from d'Arenberg is spectacular, with the nutty complex flavors of very old wine. While admittedly less expensive, the authentic port, a 20-year-old Taylor Fladgate tawny, is lacking in complexity next to the Australian version.

HAZELNUT SHORTBREAD COOKIES

These cookies are made just like shortbread, with plenty of butter and not too much sugar, except that finely ground hazelnuts are incorporated into the batter for extra flavor and to make the texture of the cookies more delicate. You can serve these cookies with all but the most delicate sweet wines, either after dinner or in the afternoon.

Makes about 60 cookies

- 1 cup hazelnuts
- 2 sticks (1/2 pound) **unsalted butter**
- 1 3/4 cups all-purpose bleached flour
- 3 tablespoons sugar
- 1 **large egg** plus **1 egg yolk**
- 1/4 teaspoon salt
  flour, for the work surface
- 1/2 **cup sugar,** for rolling the cookies

Preheat the oven to 350°F.

Spread the hazelnuts on a sheet pan and bake them until they smell toasty, about 15 minutes. If the hazelnuts still have their papery peel, rub them together while still hot in a kitchen towel. Don't worry if you don't get all of the peel.

Cut the butter in quarters lengthwise, then cut each stick (now composed of the four strips) into eight slices, giving you a total of 32 little cubes per stick, a total of 64.

Put the hazelnuts in the food processor and grind them for about a minute, until they have the consistency of coarse flour. Put the rest of the ingredients, except the flour and sugar for rolling, in the food processor with the ground nuts and process until the dough comes together in a ball, about 1 minute. Press the ball into a disk, wrap it in plastic wrap, and refrigerate it for 30 minutes.

Use both hands to roll the dough on a floured work surface into a sausage shape about 1 1/2 inches in diameter and about 20 inches long. Wrap it in plastic wrap and refrigerate for an hour or overnight.

Preheat the oven to 375°F.

Roll the sausage in granulated sugar and slice it into disks about 3/8 inch thick and arrange them on a sheet pan. Bake for 15 to 20 minutes, until the cookies are a very pale brown. Check 5 minutes into the baking to make sure the cookies are browning evenly. If not, turn the sheet pan around.

South Africa

It's hard to imagine now that during the 18th and early part of the 19th centuries, an era when sweet wines were far more revered than they are now, South Africa produced what was perhaps—with the possible exception of Hungarian Tokaji—the most famous sweet wine in the world, Vin de Constance. The best Vin de Constance was made with muscat grapes (muscat blanc à petits grains) that were allowed to shrivel to raisins in the sun, but that were not attacked by botrytis. Efforts are now being made in South Africa to bring this wine back to its original glory. International wine authority Hugh Johnson said this: "From these Elysian fields used to come one of the very greatest wines of the world. Constantia was bought by the European courts in the early 19th century in preference to Yquem, Tokay, Madeira . . . an indication that the Cape is capable of producing wines of the very highest class."

One of South Africa's most unusual wines is actually a vin de liqueur—the grape juice is combined with alcohol before it has a chance to ferment—called Jerepiko (sometimes Jerepigo). Muscat of Alexandria, less prestigious than muscat blanc à petits grains but with bigger grapes and a bigger yield, is used to make sweet wines, fortified or not, called Muscadel or Hanepoot. Other grapes, including semillon, riesling, and chenin blanc, are also used to make sweet, late-harvest wines. South Africa now has a clear labeling system. Late Harvest designates wines that are similar to German Auslese; Special Late Harvest, wines similar to Beerenauslese; and Noble Late Harvest, roughly the equivalent to Trockenbeerenauslese. South Africa also produces a number of fortified port-style wines.

VIN DE CONSTANCE

Vin de Constance (see photograph, page 119) was one of the prized wines of the world until the 19th century, when the vineyards were first attacked by oidium, a kind of mildew, and then by phylloxera, a louse that eats the vine's roots.

The winemakers have done their best to replant the same kinds of grapes, in the same locations, and under the same conditions, but the wine, while very good, isn't earth-shaking. There are, however, hints of greatness. The nose is very complex, with fragrances of spices, tropical fruit, and citrus. On the palate, under layers of muscat fruitiness, is a distinctive core of flavor that makes me think of smoke but is particularly alluring.

It's possible that as the vines get older—older vines in general make more flavorful wine—Vin de Constance will again emerge as one of the world's great sweet wines.

Left: People are always comparing wine to various fruits, but much of the time the similarity is subtle and only detectable by some. But the aroma of this Jerepiko from Rooiberg Cellars is a dead ringer for black currant liqueur—the crème de cassis used to make a kir. On the palate it tastes like a kir with a wee bit too much cassis in it. When chilled or served over ice, this inexpensive wine makes a pleasant aperitif.

MANGO WITH MINT AND VANILLA

Because mangoes aren't intensely sweet, you can get by serving them with relatively delicate and not-too-sweet sweet wines. If you're serving mango as a first course (and assuming your palate hasn't been assaulted by too many cocktails), you can match it with relatively delicate wines. Its tropical flavor is magnificent with muscat, from the delicate and lightly sparkling Moscato d'Asti to an intensely floral but vibrant Muscat de Beaumes-de-Venise, to a complex Vin de Constance. Late-harvest gewürztraminer and, if you can find one, late-harvest viognier are both great at the beginning of a meal.

If you're serving mango or other tropical fruits as dessert, choose a wine that's somewhat sweeter and more robust (because your palate will be less sensitive after eating a whole meal) such as a Sauternes or a late-harvest sauvignon blanc or sauvignon blanc–sémillon combination. (Remember, sauvignon blanc and sémillon are the two grape varieties used to make Sauternes.)

Makes 4 first-course or light dessert servings

1 bunch fresh mint
2 tablespoons sugar
1 vanilla bean
two 1-pound mangoes

Set aside four pretty mint leaves or sprigs and put the rest of the mint and the sugar in a small saucepan with 1 cup of water. Cut the vanilla bean lengthwise in half and put it in the saucepan. Bring to a gentle simmer and simmer for 5 minutes. Take out the vanilla bean—save it—and strain the mint infusion into a bowl. Scrape the tiny seeds out of each half of the vanilla bean and add them to the infusion.

Cut the mangoes in half lengthwise, sliding the knife around one side of the pit. Slice under the pit and remove it. Hold the mango half in your left hand and make horizontal and vertical slashes, about $1/2$ inch apart, down to the skin. Be careful not to cut through the skin. Cut the mango cubes where they join the skin until you've detached them all. Repeat on the other side. Chill the mango cubes and the infusion. Arrange the mango cubes in soup bowls or soup plates and spoon the mint-and-vanilla infusion over them. Decorate each serving with a sprig of mint.

THE GRAPES

I thought I knew what certain grapes tasted like until I started tasting
sweet wines. Chardonnay meant an oaky tasting Californian wine with
plenty of tropical fruit, something minerally from Chablis, or a wine
somewhere in between from Meursault or Puligny-Montrachet. Chenin
blanc meant Vouvray or one of the wines from the Coteaux du Layon.
But sweet wines sometimes capture the purity of a grape's flavor in a
way that their dry equivalents do not. If you want to taste pure grape
juice, virtually unaltered by aging and oak, try a young Canadian late-
harvest wine or an icewine made from the grape in question.

Canadian icewines aside, it's helpful to learn to recognize the flavors
of particular grapes. This knowledge will not only teach you to recognize
particular wines but also help you distinguish which qualities have to do
with the place and which are determined by the grape. Some grapes
have a very pronounced character—gewürtztraminer and viognier spring
to mind—that makes them recognizable regardless of where they are
grown and how they're made into wine. Other varietals are more malleable and have a more subtle character that reflects soil, climate, and
winemaking style instead of a pronounced varietal character.

ALBANA

Dry versions of albana, made mostly in Italy's Emilia-Romagna region, tend to lack aroma and excitement, but late-harvest passitos can be exotic and aromatic. Albana is a white grape and is sometimes called Greco or Greco di Ancona, which is not to be confused with the popular dry white wine Greco di Tufo. Albana is one of Italy's oldest documented grape varieties and was written about in the 13th century. Albana di Romagna comes in four degrees of sweetness: dry (secco), off-dry (amabile), sweet (dolce), and most sweet (passito).

ALEATICO

In his *Encyclopedia of Grapes*, Oz Clarke suggests that aleatico may be a red mutant of muscat blanc à petits grains, in part because it shares the same "heady aroma of roses." Aleatico is planted mostly in Italy in Lazio (Latium, the area surrounding Rome), Puglia (Apulia), and southern Tuscany. One of the best examples of aleatico is Aleatico di Portoferraio from the island of Elba. There are also Aleatico di Puglia and Aleatico di Gradoli from Latium. All these wines are hard to find, so nab them when you can.

CABERNET FRANC

Anyone familiar with cabernet franc and its earthy quality associates it with the great dry reds from the Loire Valley such as Chinon and Bourgeuil, so it comes as a surprise

to taste an icewine version (again, like so many unusual icewines, from Canada).

Two cabernet franc icewines are shown below. The one to the left, from Magnotta Winery in Ontario, has a restrained aroma that's almost like a dry wine with underlying hints of strawberries and blackberries. The Inniskillin cabernet franc to the right reminds me of frankincense, strawberries, and Shalimar perfume. The flavor of both is intensely sweet, with rather simple but satisfying fruit flavors and plenty of acidity to keep them from being cloying.

CHARDONNAY

For most of us, chardonnay is a soft and oaky California wine, an austere French Chablis, a French Blanc de Blancs Champagne, or, if we're really lucky, a Meursault or a Montrachet. It occurs to few of us—myself included—that chardonnay can be made into a sweet wine. A few winemakers in Italy and Austria have been making late-harvest chardonnay for years, but a good number of these wines are now made in California and Canada.

I've encountered two styles in California, a botrytized version and a fortified version. Much of the time a botrytized chardonnay is made ad hoc if botrytis has attacked the vineyards in the late fall, meaning that late-harvested chardonnay from a particular maker may not be available year-round. Fortified versions are made by adding brandy—often very fine brandy made in-house—and sugar to dry chardonnay and then aging the mixture until the flavors marry. Canadian winemakers produce both late-harvest versions and marvelous icewines that retain plenty of acidity and crisp fruit while being intensely sweet—just as sweet as a German Trockenbeerenauslese. See also Late-Harvest and Icewine Chardonnay Tasting, page 124.

CHENIN BLANC

It's rare to find a chenin blanc with any excitement made anyplace other than France's Loire Valley. California's Chappellet Winery makes a delicious, slightly oaky, sweet

RED OR PINK LENTIL SOUP

I was having dinner at a friend's house recently when the host asked me to select a wine from his collection. This can be awkward, since instinct draws one to the best bottles and the rules of restraint to something lesser. My search was complicated by our first course, a mildly spicy red lentil soup. When I took a stab in the dark and reached for a Vouvray demi-sec, I made the discovery that the gentle sweetness in the wine is the perfect match for spice.

Makes 6 first-course servings

2 **medium red onions,** chopped
4 **garlic cloves,** peeled
2 **medium carrots,** peeled and cut into 1-inch sections
4 **tablespoons butter**
2½ cups (1 pound) **red or pink lentils,** rinsed
8 cups **chicken broth** or **water**
2 tablespoons **good-quality curry powder or**
    2 **cardamom pods,** crushed under a saucepan
    2 **teaspoons ground coriander**
    ½ **teaspoon ground cinnamon**
    ½ **teaspoon ground cloves**
    ½ **teaspoon ground pepper**
    ¼ **teaspoon ground nutmeg**
    ½ **teaspoon cayenne**
one 14-ounce can **unsweetened coconut milk**
    salt to taste

Cook the onions, garlic, and carrots in 2 tablespoons of the butter in a heavy-bottomed pot over medium heat for about 20 minutes, until they become translucent and fragrant.

When the vegetables are done, stir in the lentils and add the broth or water. Bring to a simmer and simmer gently until soft, 20 to 30 minutes.

Purée the soup with an immersion blender or in batches in a regular blender. If using a regular blender, don't fill it more than halfway, and hold the lid tightly in a towel. Start by using very short pulses at the lowest speed.

Heat the curry or spices in the remaining 2 tablespoons of butter in a small pan until you smell their fragrance, 30 seconds to a minute. Stir this mixture into the soup. Stir in the coconut milk, bring to a simmer, and season to taste with salt.

Use a ladle to work the puréed vegetables and lentils through a food mill or fine mesh strainer into a clean pot and serve.

When tasting almost any wine, it's helpful to put together a small collection of closely related wines and then taste them together with a group of friends. Here are the results of tasting eight sweet chardonnays from California and Canada:

A. The people at Domaine Charbay in California have their own still and produce their own brandies, which they have not yet released because they are waiting for them to age more. (They've already waited 10 years.) This wine is made by adding their own brandy liqueur to dry chardonnay. There's a clear aroma of spirits in the nose that reminds me of a French vins de liqueur. Like vins de liqueur such as Pineau des Charentes, this fortified wine would make a great aperitif. On the palate it is quite alcoholic, but the alcohol is balanced with sweetness and fruit.

B. This Lang Vineyards Chardonnay Icewine from British Columbia has floral (I can't identify which flower) and citrus aromas in the nose that remind me of Meyer lemons and lime zests. On the palate this wine is intensely sweet, with caramel butterscotch flavors that to me signal botrytis. This wine would make an excellent stand-alone dessert or accompaniment to an apple tart, maybe a tarte Tatin.

C. Wine experts who refer to the "charcuterie nose" always left me with a suppressed giggle until I tasted this Red Rooster Winery Late-Harvest Chardonnay from British Columbia.

D. This Mission Hill Chardonnay Icewine from British Columbia has an inviting aroma of underripe blackberries followed by a crisp acidity of underripe pineapples and the flavor of overripe pineapples. Like so many Canadian icewines, this wine is beautifully balanced.

E. This Calona Vineyards Private Reserve Chardonnay Icewine from British Columbia has a crisp, lemony character and plenty of acid. It seems to have little if any botrytis, which leaves it with a clean flavor and aroma. It has an aroma of new wood that in no way dominates. It would make a delightful aperitif or accompaniment to a not-too-sweet fruit dessert.

F. You'd never guess this Domaine Combret Late Harvest Chardonnay from British Columbia was a sweet wine by smelling it—it has mineral-like lemony notes that are more reminiscent of dry chardonnay. Even on the palate this wine isn't terribly sweet but rather off-dry, which just means slightly sweet. This wine would be delicious with chicken or fish, ideally with a sauce, perhaps one containing cream. I can also imagine this wine with lightly spicy dishes—even those containing cilantro, which is difficult to pair with wine.

G. The aroma of this Lolonis Late Harvest Chardonnay "Carneros" from California reminds me of orange pekoe tea with honey in it. It tastes of pineapple or, to be more precise, pineapple wedges caramelizing in butter.

H. A slightly spicy aroma of caraway seeds coupled with lemon zests, and a clean flavor of assorted fruits that reminds me of a fruit salad with melon and watermelon, make this Paradise Ranch Chardonnay Icewine from British Columbia a lovely aperitif or accompaniment to an appetizer (prosciutto with melon or figs comes to mind).

chenin blanc, but more often than not in the New World, chenin blanc is used to make jug wines with the flavor and aroma deserving of a jug. I've read about wonderful sweet chenin blanc made in South Africa, but until I taste one I'll remain unconvinced that chenin blanc made in some other place can ever rival the chenin blanc of France's vineyards near Tours and Angers. The historic châteaux of the Loire Valley have long attracted tourists, many of whom taste French chenin blanc there for the first time. Scientists suspect that chenin blanc was a wild grape native to the Loire Valley region.

The Loire Valley can be divided into three sections. The area upstream is planted in sauvignon blanc, which, unlike the sauvignon blanc grown for Sauternes, is vinified dry into Sancerre, Quincy, and Pouilly Fume, to name a few. Most of the area downstream—Vouvray, Montlouis, Anjou, and Coteaux du Layon—is planted in chenin blanc to make both sweet and dry wines. Near the mouth of the Loire, we return to dry wines—muscadet and gros plant.

Chenin blanc, at least when grown in France, produces wines with amazingly high levels of natural acid, making the wines extremely slow-aging and able to contain relatively large amounts of sugar without seeming too sweet. In the Loire Valley, especially in the Coteaux du Layon, chenin blanc is also susceptible to botrytis, the touchstone of the Loire's greatest sweet wines. Late-harvest Vouvray is not always made from botrytized grapes, but often from grapes that have just shriveled on the vine—what the French call passerillé.

EHRENFELSER

Developed in the late 1920s, ehrenfelser is another one of those riesling-sylvaner hybrids designed to ripen more quickly than riesling itself. As in most of these situations, ehrenfelser lacks the finesse of riesling and rarely develops the acidity that make that grape so special. The best examples I've encountered are icewines from Canada (shown above right).

ERBALUCE

This obscure grape variety is thought to have originated in Italy. Erbaluce is used to make Passito di Caluso and also a small amount of dry wine. Erbaluce produces wine with a great deal of acidity, which is what makes it a good grape for making sweet wines—acidity provides essential balance to the sugar in the wine.

FURMINT

The famous Tokaji wines from Hungary (see page 87) are made from three grapes—muscat, furmint, and the unpronounceable hárslevelü. Until I discovered the California wine shown above, I had never tasted furmint on its own. This wine has soft butterscotch flavors and there are notes that remind me of Tokaji, but I probably wouldn't have made the connection had I not already known of it. While very appealing, this wine lacks the acidity of Tokaji wines and of the Chateau Pajzos muscat (see page 88).

GEWÜRZTRAMINER

Gewürztraminer seems to have originated in Italy—it's first mentioned in writings from around the year 1000—but it has since become rooted in other places, especially Alsace (where it loses the umlaut) and California.

Of all grape varieties, the flavor and aroma of gewürztraminer is the easiest to recognize because of its unmistakably distinct floral, spicy (*gewürz* is German for "spicy"), or almost candylike bouquet. (It reminds me of dried tangerine peel.) Most gewürztraminer is fermented into dry wine, but its lovely aroma and ability to ripen quickly make it a natural for turning into sweet wine. While much less commonly made into sweet wine than is riesling, gewürztraminer is made into some magnificent late-harvest wines in Alsace.

If gewürztraminer were said to have a fault, it might be that it doesn't produce enough acid. Fortunately, when gewürztraminer grapes are picked late in the year, their acid concentrates as well as their sugar, resulting in a wine that is often better balanced than it is when vinified dry. Gewürztraminer is grown in the New World, but in most places—New Zealand is the exception—the climate is simply too hot for the grapes to retain enough acidity, leaving the wine too soft.

GRENACHE

Red grenache is wildly versatile, used all over the world to make rosés (including Tavel in the south of France), in Spain (where it's called garnacha) to make Rioja, and in the southern Rhône Valley to make full-bodied Côtes du Rhône as well as more prestigious Rhône wines such as Gigondas, Lirac, and Châteauneuf-du-Pape. Grenache is such a hearty grape and when fully ripened produces so much sugar that it's a natural candidate for sweet wines. It is used in California to make a local version of port, but the best examples of a grenache sweet wine come from Rasteau and Cairanne, villages in the southern Rhône Valley best known for their dry red wines, also made from grenache.

GRIGNOLINO

Grignolino is a grape that's grown primarily in northern Italy, in the Piedmont region, to make dry, fruity red wine. It's unusual to see it in California and even more unusual to see it as a fortified wine. One of my favorite examples is from Heitz Cellars. It's much like port but with a playful fruitiness in both the nose and on the palate, a mouth-filling roundness, and a long finish. Like port, Heitz's grignolino is delicious with cheese.

PEACH OR NECTARINE BREAD PUDDING WITH WHIPPED CREAM

Come August, peaches and nectarines appear on my table, usually unadorned, at almost every meal. This bread pudding is perfect when you've lived on raw peaches for a month and want a little variation without giving up the peach. I serve it with Sauternes or Sauternes-style wines from California or Australia.

Makes 8 servings

1 1/2 cups (about 6 ounces) **walnut halves or pieces**
    4 **pounds** (about 8 large) **peaches** or **nectarines**
one 1-pound dense crumb white bread (such as Pepperidge Farm)
    2 **sticks plus 1 tablespoon unsalted butter**
1/2 **cup sugar**
    2 **cups heavy cream**
1/2 **teaspoon vanilla extract**

Preheat the oven to 350°F and toast the walnuts, spread out on a sheet pan, for about 15 minutes until they become fragrant.

Cut the peaches vertically in half, take out the pits, and cut each of the halves into 4 or 6 wedges.

Cut the crust off the bread and cut the slices into quarters so you end up with 64 squares. Melt the 2 sticks of butter in a large sauté pan and gently sauté the bread squares until they're golden brown on each side. You'll have to work in batches, rationing out the butter accordingly.

Use the remaining 1 tablespoon butter to coat a baking dish large enough to hold the bread and peaches in a layer about 2 inches thick. (I use an oval gratin dish 14 inches long and 9 inches wide at the widest point.) Cover the bottom with a layer of half the bread squares, half the peach wedges, and half the walnuts and sprinkle with half the sugar. Make another layer with the remaining bread and sprinkle over the rest of the walnuts and sugar. Cover with the rest of the peaches. Pour 1 cup of the heavy cream over the pudding.

Bake for about 1 hour, until the liquid released by the peaches almost completely evaporates and turns syrupy. Beat the rest of the cream with the vanilla and serve on the side.

SMOKED SALMON WITH YEAST-LEAVENED PANCAKES

These pancakes, called blinis, usually include buckwheat flour, which you should feel free to add. They are different from regular pancakes simply because they are leavened with yeast instead of baking powder. Pancakes cook best in a nonstick pan with no oil or butter at all. If you don't have a nonstick pan, use a minimum of butter—about a tablespoon per panful. Blinis are marvelous served with a late-harvest riesling or a demi-sec champagne.

Makes 25 pancakes (6 first-course or light main-course servings)

- 2 **cups milk**
- 1 **teaspoon active dried yeast**
   pinch sugar
- 2 **cups all-purpose flour** or 1¼ **cup all-purpose flour combined with** ¾ **cup buckwheat flour**
- 4 **large eggs**
- ¼ **teaspoon salt**
- 4 **tablespoons melted or softened butter,** for the pan (if you don't have a nonstick pan)
- 1½ **pounds cold-smoked salmon (such as Scottish or Irish)**, thinly sliced
- 1 **pint crème fraîche** or **sour cream** (to garnish)

Warm the milk in a saucepan until it feels like tepid bathwater. (If it's too hot, it will kill the yeast; if it's cold, the batter will take much longer to rise.) Combine one-fourth of the warm milk with the yeast and sugar to activate the yeast.

Combine the flour and eggs in a large mixing bowl—the batter's going to double in size—and gently work the mixture to a smooth but thick paste with a whisk. If the mixture is too stiff, work in some of the milk. When the mixture is smooth, stir in the yeast mixture and whisk in the rest of the milk until the batter has the consistency of heavy cream. Whisk in the salt. Cover the mixture with plastic wrap and let rise in a warm place until doubled in volume, about 2 hours.

Heat a large nonstick pan over medium to high heat with no butter or brush a seasoned cast-iron frying pan or omelet pan with melted or softened butter. Give the batter a quick whisking—it tends to separate during rising. Ladle the batter into the pan, making the pancakes about 4 inches in diameter. Cook the pancakes until golden brown, about 3 minutes on each side. Place them on a parchment-covered sheet pan. If you end up with more than one layer, cover the first layer with another sheet of parchment to keep them from sticking. You can make the pancakes up to a day in advance and reheat them in a 250°F oven for 10 minutes.

Place three pancakes each on heated plates, cover with two or three slices of the smoked salmon, and pass the crème fraîche or sour cream.

KERNER

Another German hybrid, kerner is designed to bud later in the spring in order to reduce the risk of the buds being killed in an unexpected frost—which would lower the yields. Kerner is supposedly widely planted in Germany, but I rarely encounter German versions in America. I have, however, found a British Columbia kerner icewine that's quite impressive.

MALVASIA

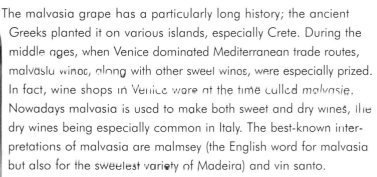

The malvasia grape has a particularly long history; the ancient Greeks planted it on various islands, especially Crete. During the middle ages, when Venice dominated Mediterranean trade routes, malvasia wines, along with other sweet wines, were especially prized. In fact, wine shops in Venice were at the time called *malvasie*. Nowadays malvasia is used to make both sweet and dry wines, the dry wines being especially common in Italy. The best-known interpretations of malvasia are malmsey (the English word for malvasia but also for the sweetest variety of Madeira) and vin santo.

Like muscat, malvasia comes in many subvarieties and colors, but most can be broken down into three basic types: malvasia bianca and its derivatives; malvasia di candia (*candia* is the old word for Crete); and the dark malvasia nera, used to produce red wines. Italian malvasia sweet wines are usually made into passito by letting the grapes dry on the vine before they are crushed and made into wine. Before World War II, malvasia wines were made throughout southern Italy and on Sardinia, but they are rarely made anymore. Malvasia delle Lipari, shown here, is made on an island off the coast of Italy; it is still available and one of the best known.

To confuse matters, the French word *malvoisie* rarely refers to malvasia, but means different things in different places. In the Loire Valley, malvoisie means pinot gris, which in Alsace, at least until recently, was called tokay. In other places in France, malvoisie refers to obscure grapes that no one outside of various small regions is likely to have heard of.

MERLOT

In combination with cabernet sauvignon, merlot is responsible for some of the world's greatest Bordeaux, especially those from St. Emillion and Pomerol. Sweet wine from merlot is very unusual, but leave it to the Canadians, who make an icewine out of just about anything, to come up with both a merlot icewine and a late-harvest merlot.

WHAT IS TOKAY?

Tokay may be the most confusing word ever used to describe wine. It is the traditional name for the great sweet wine of Hungary, now more often called by its Hungarian name, Tokaj or Tokaji. In Australia tokay refers to a grape known in most other places as muscadelle—a grape with no relation to muscat or muscadet. In Alsace tokay refers to pinot gris, a mutant of pinot noir used to produce excellent dry whites and even better dessert wines.

To complicate matters even further, tocai, sometimes called tocai friulano, is a white grape widely grown in the Friuli region of northern Italy to make dry white wine. Some experts insist that tocai is a variety of furmint, one of the grapes used to make Hungarian Tokaji, while others are convinced that tocai is sauvignon vert, a grape grown mostly in Chile.

MUSCADELLE

The most important thing to know about muscadelle is that it's not muscat. The confusion between the two is further complicated by the fact that in Spain and Portugal muscat is spelled *moscatel*. South Africa's muskadel or muscadel—both muscats—are unrelated to muscadelle.

Muscadelle is one grape that truly comes into its own in the New World, specifically Australia, where it's sometimes labeled tokay and is used to make intensely sweet, marvelously complex and dark, liqueur-style wines. (Don't confuse Australian liqueur wines with vins de liqueur—wines that have been fortified before the start of fermentation.) Muscadelle is best known in Europe as one of the wines blended in very small amounts with sémillon and sauvignon blanc to make Sauternes and Sauternes-like wines to which it contributes added aroma. Muscadelle is also used in Monbazillac, to which it gives a little whiff of smokiness

Above: This Australian liqueur tokay, made from muscadelle grapes, tastes nothing like Alsatian tokay, Hungarian Tokaji, and certainly nothing like wines made from tocai friulano. It has a deep and intensely sweet caramel flavor typical of Australian liqueur wines, which are made from blends of young and old—sometimes very old—wines that have aged in cask.

MUSCAT

Known in English and French as muscat, in Italian as moscato, in South Africa as muskadel, in Spanish and Portuguese as moscatel, and in Hungarian as muskotály, muscat is easily confused with muscadelle. To add to the confusion, there is no single grape called muscat; there are in fact over 200 varieties that range in color from pale white to darkest red. Wines are made from the muscat grape all over the world and range in quality from almost undrinkable to some of the finest of all wines.

Of all the varieties of muscat, muscat blanc à petits grains (French for "white small-berry muscat") holds the place of honor and is almost exclusively responsible for the best muscat wines. Despite the "blanc" in its name, this grape comes in colors other than white. Most of the muscat grown in Europe is white and produces wines of golden color, while much of the

Left: These five wines, all made from muscat grapes, are just a small example of the many variations in both color and flavor that can be gotten from different subspecies of muscat grapes. In order from left to right: a refreshing Moscato d'Asti, a slightly richer Muscat de Beaumes-de-Venise, a black muscat from California called Elysium, a Museum Muscat from Australia, and finally a moscatel sherry.

"GRILLED" AGED GOUDA SANDWICHES

For those of us who've tasted only young Gouda, the flavor of the hard, aged variety is striking. It has the fullness of Parmesan cheese but a distinctive flavor all its own—a nutty taste that just happens to go perfectly with a slightly sweet sherry.

When working in a restaurant where we served aged Gouda on a cheese platter, I developed an extravagant lunchtime habit. I'd make myself one of these sandwiches and down it while sipping a 40-year-old amontillado that had been sweetened into a kind of ultimate cream sherry.

Makes 4 light main-course servings

12 ounces aged Gouda or Cheddar
 8 slices dense-crumbed white sandwich bread
     (such as Pepperidge Farm)
 4 tablespoons butter

Slice the cheese and put it between the bread slices to make sandwiches. Heat half the butter in a large sauté pan (or two, if you don't have one that is big enough) and put in the sandwiches. Turn the heat to low and cover the pan. Cook for about 12 minutes, repositioning the pan(s) every few minutes so the sandwiches brown evenly. Turn the sandwiches over, add the rest of the butter, and cook them—this time without the lid so they don't get soggy—until the cheese oozes out the sides and caramelizes on the pan. Serve immediately.

muscat blanc grown in Australia and South Africa changes color from year to year (muscat is constantly mutating). The resulting wines are pink or pale red or yellow. Muscat of Alexandria is a much hardier producer than muscat blanc à petits grains, and its use in wine-making is at least as ancient. It is now grown all over the world and is especially popular in Spain. It is also the grape used to make the Portuguese Moscatel de Setúbal and the Italian Moscato di Pantelleria. Muscat of Alexandria has less aroma and finesse than muscat blanc à petits grains.

While muscat blanc à petits grains is planted all over the world, there is no one country where it predominates. In France the best-known muscat is Muscat de Beaumes-de-Venise, but white muscat is also used in the lesser-known wines of Frontignan and Rivesaltes. White muscat—moscato bianco—is also planted in Italy, where it's responsible for the cool, refreshing Moscato d'Asti and the much maligned (often justifiably so) Asti Spumante.

In the Alto Adige region of northern Italy, two kinds of muscat blanc à petits grains—goldenmuskateller and rosenmuskateller, one yellow, the other pink—are used to produce wonderful rose-scented light-bodied wines that are sold both sweet and dry. In California's Napa Valley, Mondavi wineries makes a moscato bianco that's very similar to Italy's Moscato d'Asti.

Greece's most famous wine comes from the island of Samos in three versions: Samos Doux is a vin de liqueur, essentially grape juice that's combined with alcohol so it never really ferments at all; Samos Doux Natural is a fortified wine made by adding alcohol during fermentation; and Samos Nectar, the finest, is made with raisined grapes, resulting in a wine with 14% alcohol and still plenty of sugar left.

Australia has all sorts of muscat varieties, some that are variations on muscat blanc à petits grains, others on muscat of Alexandria. The famous liqueur muscats are made from a variety called brown muscat, a type of muscat blanc à petits grains that's, well, brown.

OPTIMA

This is one of many hybrids made from riesling and sylvaner, except that it is also crossed with Müller-Thurgau in an attempt to develop a grape that ripens more quickly than riesling yet retains some of riesling's finesse. I've only heard about German versions, and never very favorably, but some interesting optima wines are made in Canada.

PINOT BLANC

Because pinot blanc was discovered in Burgundy near the end of the 19th century, it is usually compared (unfavorably) to chardonnay. But late-harvest and icewines made from pinot blanc often show more complexity than comparable wines made from chardonnay. Pinot blanc is planted in Alsace, Germany, and Austria, but the most dramatic pinot blanc sweet wines I've encountered are Canadian icewines.

Sumac Ridge Icewine from British Columbia (opposite, right) has an inviting pinelike, musky, and grassy aroma that reminds me of sauvignon blanc. With its clean, crisp flavor of ripe melon and pineapple, it's delicious as a stand-alone dessert or with something not too sweet—perhaps a ripe pear and a little Gorgonzola.

St. Hubertus Pinot Blanc Icewine, also from British Columbia (opposite, left), is crisp, refreshing, and not too sweet—a perfect aperitif. It has a clean, almost steely nose (reminiscent of German wines). This is a beautiful wine.

PINOT GRIS

To anybody who has tasted the light and refreshing pinot grigios from northern Italy, it's hard to imagine the same grape being used to make the intensely flavored late-harvest pinot gris of Alsace. Pinot gris is planted all over Europe and has become more popular among wine-makers since the 1950s, when new clones became available that yielded a relatively predictable crop.

Because pinot gris is less aromatic and distinctive than most grape varieties, it's especially good with food—it stays in the background. Pinot gris planted in Germany, where it is called ruländer, is more reminiscent of French wine, especially white Burgundy, than it is of Germany's very delicate white wines.

PINOT NOIR

Pinot noir owes its fame to the red wines of Burgundy, to French Champagne (pinot noir is a red grape, but its juice is white), and, more recently, to the wines of Oregon and California. When made in the normal way as a dry wine, pinot noir has an aroma of mushrooms intertwined in a complex tangle of red berries. Ice wine made from pinot noir has an intense aroma of fresh fruit in its purest form. It's as though the essence of the grape had been captured without any of the effects produced by the processes used for making red wine.

The aroma of the icewine shown below (from St. Hubertus Winery in British Columbia) is reminiscent of Champagne but with much more green fruit—fruit that reminds me of kiwis, blackberries, and greengage plums.

The wine is intensely sweet but with so much acidity that it still tastes irresistibly crisp and refreshing.

RIESLING

If one could name only two noble white grapes, they would be riesling and the much more appreciated chardonnay. I don't know why this great grape isn't more popular since it seems to do well in all sorts of soils and climates. Much as the great white burgundies of France are the standard-bearers for chardonnay, the magnificent rieslings from Germany and Alsace are the measure of the best late-harvest rieslings.

Riesling (pronounced reeos ling) has a couple of traits that make it especially suitable for sweet late-harvest wines. Because it has an uncanny ability to survive the cold, leaving it unaffected by sudden cold snaps, riesling can be harvested very late in the year—in a few instances even in January. Slow ripening is important for wine grapes because it gives them more time to develop flavor. Riesling also has the remarkable ability to ripen and still contain a lot of acid, which is essential to balancing the sweetness of a late-harvest wine.

Arguably the best rieslings are from Germany and Alsace, such as the two shown at right—although wine-makers from the New World have come up with some impressive competition—but there are still those who argue about the relative merits of German Rheingau and Mosel-Saar-Ruwer wines compared with Alsatian wines, which are more typically fermented dry and contain more alcohol. Comparison is difficult, however, because riesling wines made in Germany, Alsace, and the New World all have different styles.

The best German wines are slightly (or not-so-slightly) sweet, with an irresistible fragile elegance, while Alsatian wines, except some late-harvest examples, are allowed to ferment until all the sugar in the juice has been converted to alcohol. Alsatian wines taste a little like German trocken (dry) wines but usually have more body, force, and a determined mineral or steely quality. My own

favorite wines are from the Mosel or, better yet, one of the tributaries of the Mosel, the Saar or the Ruwer, where riesling grown on steep, rocky slopes has to struggle for existence (it is sometimes said that wine, like people, must struggle to develop character) because of the feeble light and the cold. The Mosel is one of the most northerly wine-growing regions in the world and produces wine with a nervous raciness that combines fruit with bright refreshing acidity and a steely mineral quality.

Late-harvest rieslings are among the New World's most promising wines. California and New York State late-harvest rieslings are sweet, but because of riesling's generous acidity, they are often beautifully balanced. They are fuller and rounder than German Rhine wines and much richer than wines from the Mosel-Saar-Ruwer. Riesling also does well in Australia (where it is sometimes labeled Rhine Riesling to distinguish it from "other" rieslings), New Zealand, and South Africa.

SAUVIGNON BLANC

Most of us associate sauvignon blanc with very dry wines from California or France, but in fact sauvignon blanc is at its dramatic best when it is blended with sémillon to make dry white Graves, sweet Sauternes, and several New World versions from Australia and California. Because sémillon produces wine with very little acidity, sauvignon blanc is used to bolster its acidity and give it a little tartness.

SCHEUREBE

This is a hybrid grape originally designed to improve the flavor of sylvaner, a popular grape in Alsace, but one that lacks the finesse of riesling. Scheurebe is now grown mostly in Germany and Austria (where it's called sämling 88). It produces wines with intense aromas and flavors, but it lacks the structure and acidity of riesling, and so scheurebe wines age more quickly than rieslings. The color of the wine shown opposite—a deep brown brought about by oxidation—lets you know that the wine has aged a bit prematurely.

SÉMILLON

Most of us have never heard of sémillon, probably because those places where it's at its best, such as Graves and Sauternes, don't put it on the label. In the Graves region of western France, sémillon is combined with sauvignon blanc to make some of the world's best dry white wines. In Sauternes and Barsac and the surrounding villages of Ste-Croix-du-Mont,

Here are three Sauternes-style wines (from left to right): Dolce from California, a Barossa from Australia, and an authentic first-growth Sauternes, Château Coutet. Tasting three wines at a time is a fascinating way to understand the subtle (and not-so-subtle) differences between wines all made in the same way from the same varietals.

I've always loved Château Coutet because, in addition to its rich sweetness, it has plenty of acid to keep it from tasting monotonous. This 1995 is classic—full of honey and butterscotch, with crispness running through it. The Dolce has a vanilla flavor—probably from new oak—that's harder to notice when it's drunk alone but stands out when it's drunk next to the Château Coutet.

The Barossa, perfectly satisfying alone, is a bit upstaged here. It smells distinctly of burnt sugar (not an unpleasant thing) and tastes a lot like bananas. All three of these wines are magnificent.

Loupiac, Cérons, and Cadillac, this same combination is used to make sweet wine.

Because ripe sémillon grapes contain very little acid, when used alone they produce a wine that tastes distinctly flat. Only when sémillon is combined with sauvignon blanc does it come into its own, the sauvignon blanc providing the necessary acidity and giving the wine much of its aroma, the sémillon providing fleshiness and, because it is very susceptible to botrytis, an intense sweetness. When this mixture of grapes is harvested late in the season, after the sémillon and to a lesser degree the sauvignon blanc are attacked by botrytis, it produces some of the greatest sweet wine in the world: Sauternes. Because Sauternes has gotten expensive, it's worth searching out similar but less costly wines from villages near Sauternes (such as the above-mentioned Ste-Croix-du-Mont, Cadillac, and Cérons) and Monbazillac from the Périgord.

In Australia, where the grape is known as semillon, excellent sweet wines are made in Hunter Valley, Eden Valley, and Riverina in New South Wales. These semillons taste little like Sauternes but rather have an identity all their own. Surprisingly for New World wines, Hunter Valley semillons contain more acid than many wines from Sauternes.

SHIRAZ

Best known by its French name, syrah, this deeply flavored red grape is the source of the great red wines—the Hermitages, Cornas, and Côte-Rôties—of the northern Rhône. These are magnificent wines, but since they are dry, we'll leave them be and move on to Australia, where syrah is called shiraz. In Australia, shiraz is used alone or in combination with grenache to make wines that often taste and smell like port. The wine shown here, from d'Arenberg in McLaren Vale, contains a lot of alcohol—you can feel it going down—and should be served slightly cool. Although it doesn't really smell like port (no such claims are made on the bottle, anyway), the nose is ripe and complex, with layers of ripe berries and other fruits. On the palate the wine tastes very concentrated (you can also see this by its deep color), and its structure—the balance of fruit and alcohol—reminds me of port, although the flavors themselves are different, more like a combination of hay and ripe fruit.

VIDAL

This is a French hybrid grape that's used mostly in Canada to make icewines. Like riesling, vidal stands up well to the cold, making it perfect for the Canadian winters, but it doesn't produce wines with quite the finesse of those made from riesling. In all honesty, though, I often have a hard time tasting the difference.

VIOGNIER

This grape, traditionally grown for dry white wines in the village of Condrieu, in France's Rhône Valley, has a floral and spicy perfume and low acidity that lends wines an impression of sweetness even when they contain very little sugar. Lately, viognier has become stylish and is used in many parts of the world to produce soft, immediately drinkable dry whites and occasionally late-harvest sweet wines. Late-harvest Condrieu, rare and expensive, shows viognier at its best. As explained on the label, this wine is made from grapes that have raisined (passerille) on the vine and grapes that have been affected by botrytis (pourriture noble). The nose reminds me of a flower garden with a distinct aroma of artichokes. On the palate there's very little of the characteristic butterscotch flavor of botrytis, but the wine is round and rich and floral. It's too delicate and not sweet enough to serve with dessert and a bit too sweet to serve as an aperitif. Try serving it in the afternoon with a cookie or the Ladyfingers on page 92.

BUTTER ALMOND COOKIES (FINANCIERS)

These cookies make a great afternoon or after-dinner snack with a glass of sweet sherry, Madeira, or riesling.

Makes about 30 cookies

12 tablespoons butter
 2 cups confectioners' sugar
³/₄ cup plus 2 tablespoons blanched almonds, toasted for 10 to 15 minutes in a 350°F oven and allowed to cool
¹/₃ cup plus 1 tablespoon flour
 5 large egg whites
 2 tablespoons softened butter (for the molds)

Preheat the oven to 450°F.

Melt the 12 tablespoons of butter in a heavy-bottomed saucepan over medium heat. It will boil for about 10 minutes while the water cooks out of it and then it will start to froth. At this point you must watch it carefully so you caramelize the milk solids without burning them. Tilt the pan so you can see the milk solids clinging to the bottom. As soon as they turn brown, plunge the bottom of the pan in a bowl, stirring of cold water for a few seconds to stop the cooking but not so long that the butter congeals.

Combine the sugar and almonds in a food processor and grind for about 2 minutes. Combine the almond mixture with the flour and egg whites in a mixing bowl, stirring with a wooden spoon until smooth. Work in the melted butter and refrigerate the batter for at least an hour—preferably overnight—before baking.

Brush the financier molds or 1-inch tartlet molds with a layer of softened butter. Chill the molds for 10 minutes and brush again. They must be very thickly coated with butter or the financiers will stick. Spoon the batter into the molds (or use a pastry bag), filling them about three-quarters of the way up (the mixture expands). Put the molds on a sheet pan and slide them into the oven. Bake for 5 minutes, turn the oven down to 400°F, and bake for 6 to 7 minutes more until the cookies are brown on top. Let cool for 1 minute before unmolding onto a rack.

CONVERSION CHARTS

WEIGHT EQUIVALENTS

The metric weights given in this chart are not exact equivalents, but have been rounded up or down slightly to make measuring easier.

Avoirdupois	Metric
¼ oz	7 g
½ oz	15 g
1 oz	30 g
2 oz	60 g
3 oz	90 g
4 oz	115 g
5 oz	150 g
6 oz	175 g
7 oz	200 g
8 oz (½ lb)	225 g
9 oz	250 g
10 oz	300 g
11 oz	325 g
12 oz	350 g
13 oz	375 g
14 oz	400 g
15 oz	425 g
16 oz (1 lb)	450 g
1½ lb	750 g
2 lb	900 g
2¼ lb	1 kg
3 lb	1.4 kg
4 lb	1.8 kg

VOLUME EQUIVALENTS

These are not exact equivalents for American cups and spoons, but have been rounded up or down slightly to make measuring easier.

American	Metric	Imperial
¼ t	1.2 ml	
½ t	2.5 ml	
1 t	5.0 ml	
½ T (1.5 t)	7.5 ml	
1 T (3 t)	15 ml	
¼ cup (4 T)	60 ml	2 fl oz
⅓ cup (5 T)	75 ml	2½ fl oz
½ cup (8 T)	125 ml	4 fl oz
⅔ cup (10 T)	150 ml	5 fl oz
¾ cup (12 T)	175 ml	6 fl oz
1 cup (16 T)	250 ml	8 fl oz
1¼ cups	300 ml	10 fl oz (½ pt)
1½ cups	350 ml	12 fl oz
2 cups (1 pint)	500 ml	16 fl oz
2½ cups	625 ml	20 fl oz (1 pint)
1 quart	1 liter	32 fl oz

OVEN TEMPERATURE EQUIVALENTS

Oven Mark	F	C	Gas
Very cool	250–275	130–140	½–1
Cool	300	150	2
Warm	325	170	3
Moderate	350	180	4
Moderately hot	375	190	5
	400	200	6
Hot	425	220	7
	450	230	8
Very hot	475	250	9

INDEX

(Page numbers in *italic* refer to photographs)

FOOD AND RECIPE INDEX

(Page numbers in *italic* refer to photographs)